Nurse Specialist

The Good, the Bad and the Privilege

A personal memoir of a career in nursing.
Heartwarming and equally heartbreaking,
sprinkled with laughter

By

Annie Salter

Copyright © Annie Salter, 2024

All rights reserved. No part of this publication may be reproduced or transmitted without the express permission of the author.

ISBN: 9798340709639

This book is the personal recollections of real events. The permission of the patients or patients' families has been obtained to share their stories. Where this was not possible, the personal details of the individuals have been changed in order to protect their anonymity.

Cover Design by L. Gibbons

Titles also by the same author

Tide's Reach
Sweet Revenge

Review by Former Patient

These memoirs are a truly inspirational account of a nurse's journey from training to retirement.

It is a must read for all young nurses to understand the importance and dedication needed to become a caring, empathetic and knowledgeable practitioner. It shows the incredible battle that nurses face through trials and tribulations, frustration about the system but most importantly it gives a real insight into the rewards and emotions the job provides.

The sadness and heart ache are also acknowledged yet the resilience and perseverance to make a difference is overwhelming.
I truly recommend this book as a read both to nurses and patients.

Gill Millett

Personal Note.
I would like to thank Gill for taking the time to read my manuscript and writing the above book review. You were a pleasure to nurse and you are a fabulous ally on the committee.

Annie

Dedication

This book is dedicated to my parents, who taught me the values of being a nurse.

To all those fabulous nurses I have worked with over the years: you know who you are.

To all the patients, who can recall the best, and the worst of the profession.

Lastly, to any brave enough to take up the challenge and become a nurse, good luck you will need it.

Nurse Specialist

The Good, The Bad and The Privilege.

A memoir by Annie Salter

Contents

Chapter Title	Page
Title Page	1
Contents	2
Introduction	3
Day One	9
Intro-block	16
Wellbeing	34
Orthopaedics	42
See How You Like It	71
Photos 1 to 7	95
Death	100
Living With Nurses	105
Midwifery	117
Achilles Heel	127
Resuscitation	137
Cancer	149
Photos 8 to 16	167
Perks	176
Mental Health	184
Being a CNS	206
Endoscopy	220
The Other "C" Word	230
Curses	243
Things That Stay With You	255
Conclusion	260

Introduction

In the peace and tranquillity of retirement I contemplate the big question, to revalidate or not to revalidate. Nursing now dictates that every three years you must prove you have worked enough hours, and spent enough time in training to demonstrate you are still competent. Your daily grind and annual subscription to an anonymous nursing body that gives you nothing in return is no longer enough.

The decision will come in April 2025 when I will have to decide - is it time to let it go and hang up my stethoscope? Once relinquished my nursing qualification, experience and the right to practice evaporates and I can legally nurse no more.

I have wanted to write my rambled recollections for many years in an attempt to capture the essence of the most privileged of all professions. The role of a nurse has on the surface changed dramatically over the 37 years that I have witnessed, but intrinsically it remains the same. By way of inspiration, I have read many old books and articles on nursing dating back to the 1700s, and fundamentally nothing has changed. In an effort to convey what makes a good nurse I looked at the old texts. These talk of the traits of a good nurse and these I think are still as pertinent today. Some may take exception to the language but a nurse should be clean, kind, courageous, gentle and efficient. It may not be sexy or high tech but it is so true.

Times may have changed but sickness has not. For all of the technological advances patients now live for longer, usually having amassed more illnesses and chronic conditions until the inevitable occurs. The only true certainty is we will all die, and that folks, is as old as time. Pain is still the same, prolonged pressure kill cells leading to pressure sores. Illness is undignified and frightening, and that is true for every person on the planet. It truly is the one universal truth, and caring for someone who is sick is likewise the same everywhere.

For the purposes of this book, I will refer to the nurse as she/her, only because the vast percentage are. Before the woke police start, my father was a nurse and a bloody wonderful one. As for your sexual orientation, colour, or what you identify as, I don't care. This my friends, is the first basic rule of nursing – it doesn't matter.

Knowledge of religious practice, dietary considerations and treatment of the dead are aspects that affect care and should be taught and learnt. Religions have rules and as medical professionals, we respect them.

Blood is the same colour in all of us, urine is the same (no extra brownie points for saying not in a jaundiced patient), faeces are always offensive, especially if smeared up your arm. Pain doesn't care who you sleep with, cancer doesn't care if you identify as a different sex and a ruptured appendix will be treated the same if you are a murderer or a king. If you are not medically trained it may be a revelation, that medicine is not biased, nor ever should be. So, if I offend anyone's fragile sensibilities, sorry, but maybe stop reading now.

A good nurse will always introduce herself to a patient thus; "Hello my name is Anne and I am going to be looking after you, what would you like me to call you?" Tell me your name and I will use it, tell me who is important to you and I will keep them informed and supported.

I certainly didn't need to wear a badge or wear a rainbow lanyard to support diversity in the NHS, whoever proposed this has missed the bloody point! I did ask (facetiously) the hospital if we could have a grey lanyard to support the heterosexual, menopausal, arthritic nurses, and lo and behold there was a menopause awareness day – the irony is too much, enough said.

Sadly, gone are the days when stately old consultants and fearsome matrons ran a hospital with intelligence, understanding and rationality. Now youngsters with business degrees, accountants and corporate numpties with no understanding of the dynamics in medicine, dictate the terms. These terms are budgets, money over medicine and profits over people (patients and staff). Little wonder the NHS and its staff are on their knees.

I will recount my experiences and a few of the thousands of patients I have had the privilege to nurse. The gratification of working so intimately with a complete stranger and gaining their absolute trust is a job like no other. Memories of a myriad of encounters are tattooed in my heart and mind, and I will share just a few with you in the following pages.

I will try to capture the tools you need to succeed, and the character traits that help you continue in what is a punishing career. These tools are skills we carry to make a nurse caring and efficient.

I am exceptionally proud to be a third-generation nurse, following in the footsteps of my paternal grandfather and both my parents and have strived to conduct myself always with as much kindness, compassion and good humour as I could muster. I hope you enjoy the insight into a truly unique job

Skills are honed over years of experience, minutiae of communication, verbal or non-verbal are the bedrock of a skilled nurse. The ability to observe, hearing what is said and not said, capturing a seed of a question, a darted look, the sign of the fear or anxiety someone is too afraid to voice. There is an understanding of when to talk and when to listen and more importantly the time for silence. Adapting language to match the understanding of a patient, who to call 'sir' and who to call 'mate'. Reading the dynamic and following the lead of the patient to use humour to get through a difficult discussion and when this is wholly inappropriate.

Touch can be a powerful tool in comforting, reassuring and connecting with the patient. As with everything in nursing it is judged case-by-case and evaluated continually. If I put my hand on yours and you pull back minutely, I would retract mine. If my hand is grabbed by both the patient and the relatives, it is a clear sign that they are tactile people and will gain comfort and support from that small act of kindness. In a society where teachers can't hug a crying child luckily, not yet anyway, we are still allowed to touch our patients and should appreciate the value of it.

I have written some fiction and write for enjoyment having no formal training so the quality, relevance or value of this I leave to you the reader to decide. I'm a nurse, what do I know?

Day one

Young nurses like teenagers will always bemoan the older generation for thinking that they know best; sadly, for nursing this is true. The phrase "In my day" will always illicit complaints of how out of touch and old fashioned you are. Now nurses have degrees, they go to university which means £9000 a year in fees. Working for nothing on placements on the wards, they usually have to hold down second jobs to try to cover their cost of living and debt. Let me tell you how it was in 'my day'. I can hear the grinding of teeth and the raising of young eyebrows. Yes, I did just say that, but hear me out and then judge me wrong.

I was 18 and my Morris Minor groaned under the weight of all my essentials to start my new life in Epsom Hospital nurse's home. I very nearly didn't make it. Seeing my mum and brother disappear in the rear-view mirror didn't make leaving home easy. For the next hour and a half, I cried. No gentle, wistful cry, this was full on sobbing and at the Devil's Punch Bowl, choking and spluttering on snot and tears, the little grey Minor mounted the curb and all four wheels bounced along the embankment.

By the time I arrived at the car park I was a shaken soggy mess. Adrenaline fuelled by fear, I desperately scanned the site. To my immediate relief I spotted an estate car with two parents upfront and the young girl peering out from amongst a portable TV, small fridge and numerous boxes. So, my first friend was found, and I stalked them until they parked and hurried to follow them.

I had visited Epsom only once for an interview so had no idea where I was going. I had wanted to be a chiropodist but misspent weekends at the beach and the pub in the first flush of love, I had missed my A-level grades. The chiropody school said unfortunately now the entry requirement had changed, but if I would like to take A-level Chemistry in a year I could defer. So here I was, the one thing I always said I didn't want to be, a student nurse. At my school career day my humanities teacher said "Be a nurse!" My tutor, beloved man to me said, "Be a nurse!" The one person who didn't was my mother. She had met my father whilst they trained to be nurses and knowing the immensity of the challenge she said "Don't do it, it is too hard, and too sad". When I asked her why both my parents had chosen that profession, she had to admit it is the best job you can do.

The Chiropody door was now firmly closed to me as the thought of doing A-level Chemistry in any amount of time seemed totally unobtainable and distasteful. Katie was a Vicar's daughter whom I had met at college, when we sat together for our biology classes. As she had gone to start her nurse training at Epsom it seemed to be the place to go. I never considered my local hospitals and never questioned that decision. Now I think it was less about wanting to be a nurse than wanting to fly the nest and have an adventure.

My parents were both trained at Hackney hospital. (See photo1) They had started their nurse training together in the 1950s when the NHS was new and shiny. (See Photo 2) So in my 18-year-old logic I would follow their footsteps back to my East End roots. I had interviews at four London hospitals, all equally terrifying. I had grown up in a small town in Hampshire and the hustle and grime of the city felt unfriendly and intimidating, so Epsom seemed a good compromise, and with little thought I was here.

With my father long since dead and a mother who couldn't drive it made sense for me to load all my possessions and go off alone. This was a mistake, not only because of the near-death experience, but the red swollen face I could do nothing to rectify.

I followed the highly made-up glamorous girl and her parents I had stalked in the car park. Entering the education centre, conveniently located at the bottom of the nurse's home, I kept them in sight but hung back lacking the gumption to actually talk. Lecturers and nurses in uniform were there to greet us, a room of young girls and their parents. I, feeling like Oliver Twist with my swollen, tear-stained face had neither the courage nor the confidence to talk to anyone but stood in the corner and shakily sipped my orange juice. Standing there I don't think I have ever felt so alone.

I can't recall who talked, or what they told us as I was too busy frantically scanning the dozen or so other girls. All about my age and all in the protection of their families, I was trying to decide who would be my new friends. I remember a little boost to my beleaguered confidence as they all had to say farewell to their families. I had done that already and with a deep breath and shy smiles we were taken on a tour.

The nurse's home was to be our abode for the next three years and three months. The housing officer was an officious and unfriendly woman who assigned the rooms to the newest intake of students. It was a Victorian building comprised the school, with library and classrooms and an array of offices on the ground floor. (See Photo 3) Shaped like a wide letter 'H' there were three floors above comprising rooms, or cells for nurses to occupy. Each one had a sink, limited electrical supply and a six-foot draughty sash window.

And so, the sad procession began, walking from one of the long drab corridors to another, depositing nurses as we went. We were spread-out, over-all floors and corridors. The housing officer would open the door, pushing it wide then consulting her book, and without so much as a smile, would call a name, hand them the key and swiftly move on. The group was dwindling and I tried hard to remember door numbers so I might find them again. But as every large dark door slammed my hopes faded, I would never remember.

We were down to the last three, when on the third floor, down an as yet unexplored corridor, my name was called. The heavy door opened to a room that had nothing to recommend it. The odour of old shoes and curry was ingrained in the dark orangey brown carpet worn to a sticky sheen. The walls were dirty dull pink set off by orange striped curtains. A single metal framed bed with a mattress (I didn't want to sit on, let alone sleep on), and a beaten-up chest of drawers were the only furniture. Not wanting to stay any longer, I walked back along the long corridor, opened and slammed the two heavy concertina lift doors and went out to my car. The temptation to get in and drive back to the love and safety of home was, at that point, a real and considered option. But taking a few deep breaths, my kettle and as many bags as I could carry, I headed back in. Sadness growing with each trip in the lift, an ancient clattering beast, and then the lonely trudge of the longest corridor to my new home. Anywhere less like home couldn't be imagined, and the tears started and continued to stream.

  The car park by the entrance was frenetic, mums and dads unloading, laughter and arguing, and me. It took many trips but finally I was in. My entertainment package comprised a tiny TV with four channels and a cassette radio. I had six tapes and Clannad became the soundtrack for my despair, I sat on the floor and cried some more. It was only hunger that composed me and drove me from my horrid room.

Two girls who had seemed friendly had been deposited on the second floor. They had adjacent rooms near the fire doors in the middle of the long corridor. I hadn't been wrong and couldn't remember any of the room numbers, but I did remember the location. I mustered my last speck of bravery; there was nothing for it, I was going to have to knock and find them. I trotted down the cold concrete staircase to the second floor. Stretching out before me through three sets of fire doors I could see the back of three of the girls with one of their fathers walking with them, they were nearly at the other end by the lift. In a memory so ingrained in my mind, I can remember now the utter panic of "I must get to them" which without thought made me sprint; only to be stopped in my tracks by "What if they don't want me to go out with them, maybe they're already friends and wouldn't want me tagging along?" I forced myself to run and impose myself on these girls and they welcomed me and to my eternal gratitude are still my dearest friends today. (See photo 4)

Intro block

The first six weeks were spent in school, known as introductory block, where all the basic skills were taught. You were part of a 'set', a class of a dozen student nurses who would stay together for the entirety of your training. (See Photo 5) We lifted (a hoist was a thing of dreams in the 1980s), we injected peaches and took blood pressures over, and over, and over again. The tutors were fabulous and learning intense and they were to be our guides, educators and role models for the next three years. Our future was mapped out in blocks; we would work full-time on a ward for eight to ten weeks, followed by one or two, weeks full-time block of learning in the classroom. Each block covered a specific subject i.e. cardiology, respiratory, anatomy etc, and the end of each week there were always exams, which had to be passed. Then as a group we were let loose again onto the wards. Each one had set assignments and workbooks pertinent to the speciality again which had to be passed.

Here I would like to introduce you to my top ten (there must have been so many more) idiotic ideas made by the nursing profession. Now, I have never been shy of saying, I told you so. I would like to record for posterity the ideas that have been forced on the profession, which at the time I called 'Bullshit'. So come on down idiotic idea number one, which is without doubt in my mind the leading reason for the decline in our profession; welcome the University degree.

It was dictated that to raise the profession to the ranks of similar specialities i.e. dentistry, medicine and law, nurses should no longer be taught in a hospital but join the ranks of those at university. Did it? Of course not! Comparatively nothing has changed we still earn less, work harder and have nothing positive to show for it. What the poor nurse of today does have, is a massive debt, inadequate practical training and the highest burnout and retention drain there has ever been before.

The seismic shift of taking the students off the wards for the majority of their training left a gapping hole. Auxiliaries/HCSW now do the bulk of the hands-on care. We learnt on every ward for three years the basics of care in all specialities, but now student nurses have a small taster. The auxiliaries work load and responsibilities have rocketed (With no professional body for protection or adequate training). Student nurses experience is limited and their knowledge is often inadequate. The real victim here is the patient.

Prior to requiring a university degree nurses lived and learned on site, all they needed to know was imparted by the staff in the hospital that employed them. Although it was a full-time practical course there was constant studying. Living above the library and being able to pop down in your slippers to research an essay (there was no google then), and a walk to work of 30 seconds were priceless. An aspect of nurse training that was totally disregarded and undervalued when they closed hospital schools of nursing and made nurses study at universities.

Medical interventions have grown exponentially; technology is king and you now need a password and an app to record a blood pressure or dish out an aspirin. Standards have slipped, and every basic care requires a complex flow diagram and algorithm because staff are either, not able, or not trusted to just do their job. I fear they have evolved to bridge the gapping void of understanding that is the result of teaching nurses, not on the ward but in an academic setting far removed from a patient.

I constantly struggle not to be negative about the state of the profession I love, but I will try my best. A good nurse doesn't need a flowchart to tell her a patient is unwell; a touch of a forehead will tell you if there is a fever. In an attempt to maximise professionalism by taking nurses from the wards to learn in university, they have deprived the profession of its very core essence. All these things can be taught in principle in a classroom, but nothing compares to watching and learning from experienced colleagues who should explain why and how they have tackled the care they give.

Those first six weeks spending every day in class together and socialising at night formed strong and supportive friendships. A few nurses chose not to live in and missed out on a lot. Again, the value of this was grossly under rated. We didn't talk about mental health issues or well-being then. Honestly a sympathetic shoulder to cry on, a cup of tea or cheap sparkling wine was always available and got us all through some very tough times.

Then came the day! The first day you donned the uniform, the chequered dress, thick stockings and very unattractive lace up rubber soled shoes. None of which are apparel to be proud, but top it off with a belt and a paper hat and you felt ten feet tall. We all proudly pinned our fob watches to our chests and clutched our small notepads and pens. There was a pride that day that has never left me, but was then accompanied by utter terror.

There was a clear hierarchy, first years had one blue stripe on their hat, second years, two stripes and third years, yes you guessed it, three stripes. As a chicken owner I know the callousness of a pecking order and nurses are no different. First years get all the bedpans to empty and cleaning jobs, as you progress you delegate the menial smelly jobs to someone junior to you. There was no such thing as fair in nursing, you did the grotty jobs and bided your time until you could get someone else to do it for you.

There is a little-known disease that can affect nurses, it happens as they qualify and become a staff nurse. After spending three years being told what to do, they can be affected by 'Staff Nurseitis', suddenly they can sit at a desk and dish out the crappy jobs. For most it is a temporary state, but there are nurses out there who perpetuate this their whole career, and often end up in senior roles.

Nursing is a hard job. There is just no other way to define it or flower it up. We had a saying 'If it's too hard, work in Marks and Spencer's, the pay and the food are better.' Patients have a raft of needs, and on every shift you cannot pre-empt or plan, because every day and every patient is different. This not only makes every day a challenge but it is what ultimately makes it so rewarding.

After a couple of weeks came our first visit to meet an actual patient. I think with hindsight this was planned to thin the pack, weed out the weak and save investing any more time on those who wouldn't stay the course. All dressed in our crisp uniforms we squeaked our way over the car park into the back entrance of the hospital. This staff entrance via the morgue door had us all self-consciously fiddling with our hats; which although held on with a dozen hair clips felt it could slip or blow off at any moment, when in fact they never moved.

Before I get to the patient, I must address hats, we wore hats proudly, they served three main purposes;
One, it didn't matter what your hair looked like because every last hair had to be dragged back and secured underneath it.
Two, once positioned in the morning it could happily stay in place. Many is the time I've gotten into bed still with my hat securely attached.
Three, most importantly, any patient, no matter how confused or drowsy can see a smiling face looking down with a hat, and instantly, universally, recognise a nurse.

Sorry to digress we will get to the patient in a moment, but bear with me. To celebrate 50 years of the NHS the hospital I worked in had asked for volunteers to wear period uniforms for the day. I jumped at the chance, with crisp white linen aprons and hats which I took home and dutifully washed and starched whilst my mum regaled me with her reminisces of actually having to work in them. (See Photo 6) Amongst the women who joined me in the celebration were matrons, heads of nursing and the chief executive, who was herself once a nurse. It was with great delight I informed most of them

"Poor show nurse, your hat is a disgrace!" (See Photo 7).

I spent my working day in full uniform in an endoscopy unit, working in the reception of the department that could put a camera in any bodily orifice. With no amateur dramatic experience, I inhabited the role with enthusiasm. In true method acting, I was a 1950s nurse, I had taken tips from my mother and from stories I had heard her tell. Consultants were called 'Sir' which of course they liked too much, and colleagues were called by their surname. There was zero tolerance for any impropriety and much fun was had by all, well, with the exception of a poor student nurse who came from the ward to collect her patient.

"You need to go and wash that muck off your face and get all this hair cut off or clipped back!" The look of horror on her face was proof she had no idea I was in character. Sadly, with a heavy heart I had to apologise, when deep down I pined for the days when we had such standards.

Hats were done away with soon after I qualified – how dare they! Just as I was about to step up to the lace pill box hat of a staff nurse, they took them away. The rationale was that they were an infection risk, which of course is quite the contrary and we shall call this idiotic idea number two. Once you had pinned your cap in place there was no need to touch it, or your hair again for the rest of your shift. Without hats hair now is loose and unrestrained and still to this day I mourn the loss of hats. I watch nurses brushing back their hair that falls over their shoulders, or pushing it behind ears, not to mention into a patient's dinner or an open wound.

Don't get me started on false eyelashes and fake nails. It's a beauty pageant now apparently, infection control and standards be damned.

The real reason we should never have done away with the crowning glory of our uniform was highlighted on that day. In full vintage uniform with my crisp apron and billowing hat I welcomed a patient to reception. She was frail and afraid, clinging and rattling the trolley bars, she moaned and cried. Whatever form of dementia afflicted her she took no comfort from the porters and nurses in scruffy surgical scrubs around her. From across the room, she saw me and reached out her hand, "Nurse, a nurse, HELP ME!"

In the theatrical costume, through the confusion of her mind she saw me, she knew what I was, she trusted I would help her. I held her hand

and she kissed it. I accompanied her and comforted her throughout her stay and during the procedure. Deep within us is an innate trust and un-said knowledge that nurses are there to help and protect. Decades after losing my hat I felt vindicated that I had been right all along.

Sorry for the detour, back to the ward and our first foray into being a real nurse. Separated into smaller groups we arrived on the ward, my gaggle (what is the collective noun for nurses I wonder? A pride? A herd? – no I like gaggle). Were taken to a surgical ward, here a third-year student took us into a stuffy single room where a mildly terrified young man sat in the bed in his pants and T-shirt. The patient was only a little older than us and had sustained a nasty leg injury from a motorbike accident. Running down his hairy lower leg was an 8-inch wound with thick black stitches/sutures. Dissolving sutures were a thing for the future, these were good old fashion thick black twine.

Our guide, a bubbly talkative Irish girl, told us she was going to remove his sutures. Blushes coloured everyone in the room including our poor patient. Soon after the first stitch was out one of our number had to sit down, and one ran from the room covering her mouth. I think the fact that this patient had been chosen was due to his over healed, mucky wound and the fact that the poor young man involved was clutching his bedsheets and pleaded for it all to be over. It was a short sharp test of our mettle. Not only was it a taste of the blood and guts side of nursing but also the strange new sensation that you, will as a nurse, control the fate of others. The dawning realisation that your job entailed seeing, and touching, sometimes attractive, often abhorrent people in their pants or less.

There had been a long tradition in nursing and one I fell foul of in my first official shift on a ward. With a straight face the ward sister instructed me to go to the adjoining ward to get something for her. My desire to please, succeed and fit in, were only matched by my pure terror, so off I went. Feeling slightly nauseous I stood at the nurse's station of the Gynae ward next door.

"Hello, I'm from Alex ward, I've been asked to come and get a long stand?"

I remember the sister looking at me for cringe worthy seconds then answering.

"Right...wait there" pointing at the end of the desk. No one seemed to be looking for the item I had been sent for, and a constant internal battle of

'You've been off your ward for too long' versus, 'Utter fear of speaking to that sister again' resulted in my quietly waiting.

After what seemed like hours, but was probably a few minutes the sister looked up, her face deadpan "That's it, you've had your long stand".

To the sound of staff sniggering, I hurried back to my ward. Was this bullying? Today's sensibilities would see it so. I was just relieved as I hadn't fallen for. 'Go to the operating theatre to get and ask for some fallopian tubes!'

This brings me neatly onto medical humour. To survive in medicine, whether you are a doctor, nurse or allied health professional, one of your greatest weapons is humour. It is the tool you should keep polished and ready to use when appropriate. It is not a slapstick or jokey humour; it is usually a dark and often deeply inappropriate one. Things are discussed and comments made that can never leave an office.

The last hospital I worked in used to have an annual review; a show performed by staff for the enjoyment of staff. A very talented intensive care consultant with a ukulele accompanied by a band of frustrated performers covered topics ranging from necrophilia to blow-up sex dolls and generally ripping apart all that was stupid and idiotic – usually aimed squarely at hospital managers. It was at the time a certain health minister was attempting to scupper doctor training. A very well received sketch based on a rhyming quiz show had a packed local theatre with hundreds of NHS staff – in unison – with deafening volume, shouted a word that rhymes with Hunt.

Patients would have been shocked, if the press got wind of it there would have been a national outcry. Yet I was proud, proud to be part of the biggest unified profession, all sharing a humour like this, that gets you through.

One of my least favourite memories, of which I am almost too ashamed to share happened on a long, old fashioned Nightingale style ward. The door to the ward led first to the sister's office, equipment rooms, sluices and bathrooms. From there you could look down the length of the ward to the day room or lounge at the end. 15 beds down each side with the occupants looking at the patient opposite. Of course, then they were single sex wards, meaning either all-male or all-female. This was a good thing as barring a thin curtain (these were always pulled back unless washing, toileting, nakedness and death - privacy was not an option) every sniff and fart could clearly be heard. Visibility for the staff was invaluable, and a quick scan could check every patient.

Now-a-days small isolated rooms contain four or six patients who can now dictate the terms and choose to sit behind closed curtains. I am all for patient choice but if you are quietly choking or bleeding to death from a disconnected drip, no one is going to see you. Safety should always trump everything else.

I was working on a female medical ward with mainly respiratory patients. This basically means much coughing and sputum. A fast-learning curve on helping someone struggling to breathe, and the safe administration of oxygen. One such patient had died in her sleep, at lunch time, in her bed right in the middle of the ward. The curtains had been pulled and as always, a hush washed over the other patients as bed-to-bed the ripples spanned out. They all knew a fellow patient had died and in silent contemplation were inevitably wondering if they were next. There was always a shifting hierarchy of the sickest patients being placed nearest the Sister's office. You wanted them close to keep an eye on them and should they need attention or sadly die they are near the exit and you can save the other patients the procession of the metal coffin down the length of the ward.

I would like to justify myself before I go on. I was unable to complete my science exam at school because when I am nervous, I giggle. Not a titter or small chuckle, but a face morphing hysteria. So, my presentation on 'life on the oil rigs' never got past the title, and despite a few attempts and stints in the school corridor my poor teacher admitted defeat and let me sit it out. Abject apologies to the patient and fellow onlookers but when I am nervous, I laugh, often inappropriately, often uncontrollably.

So back to the ward and the dearly departed. The doctor had seen her and certified she was in fact dead. The family had spent their last moments with her and now it was time for the 'laying out'. The expression 'see one, do one, teach one' sums up medicine, there is little point watching over and over again and the sooner you get on and do things it can be added to your tool box.

I had seen one dead body have last offices as it is known, so felt ready to tackle it myself. Although still only a first year, I relished any opportunity to take under my wing and impart some knowledge to a limp looking first warder. So, we prepared our trolley, the pack with the shroud and sheets, relevant paperwork and a bowl of hot soapy water. With appropriate solemnity we walked slowly past the sad faces and small nods of the remaining ladies. You could literally have heard a pin drop. Very quietly I proceeded to reassure and talk through what we were about to do as we closed the curtains back around us. I remembered and reiterated what the sister had said to me when I had watched her.

"This is your final act of kindness, treat the patient as if they were still alive, just sleeping."

With the young nurse (probably 18 like myself) on the other side of the bed we began to give the last bed bath. In days when you had time and what's more, a proper bowl and flannel there was an art to bed bathing. Towels and sheet covered all areas not being washed maintaining dignity by limiting exposure and keeping the patient warm. These steps were honoured even with our now cold corpse, I washed and my counterpart dried. She was rather pale and wide-eyed, the nurse that is! But I was confident we would get through this.

"That's it nice and gentle, right let's turn her and we'll wash her back," hushed words of reassurance. If you have never seen a dead body, it is amazing how quickly they change and this lady was cold and waxen, which alone can be quite daunting for two young nurses to deal with. On the count of three, under my direction we rolled the deceased away from me. My colleague's role at this point was to have her forearm nearest the patient's head behind the shoulders and the other hand supporting the hips, thus keeping her on her side so I might wash her back. It happened in a flash.

As we pulled and pushed simultaneously two things happened, a rush of air escaped the body exiting as a moan. Neither of us knew this was a normal occurrence so unsurprisingly we reacted badly. I froze, open-mouthed, whilst my colleague swore loudly and leapt backwards. I too may have stepped back, but being mid back wash found my arms pinned to the bed under the weight of the dead body. Being acutely aware that the whole affair would be heard by our silent audience I hushed the nurse and whispered for her to come and help, and then it happened -my nervous laugh. If you are lucky enough in life to have experienced hysterical laughter you will know there is no control. So, there

I was desperately trying to suppress a tidal wave of raucous laughter behind curtains with a dead body and a traumatised baby nurse, surrounded by a ward of hushed patients listening to our every word.

I tried coughing, clamping my hand over my mouth, and even pain inflicted by painfully pinching myself, all to no avail. We stayed hidden behind the curtain much longer than the job warranted. When I finally decided I had to leave it was a rush to the nearest bathroom covering my face. Some people turn to drink or drugs but my reflex to stress is laughter. This was absolutely not my finest hour.

Wellbeing

Wellbeing and mental health are the current buzz words, never more so than today it seems. We are bombarded with the state of everyone's mental health. The stiff upper lip has never been so feeble and tremulous. I think back to my parents who survived being evacuated as children in WW2. Working 70hr weeks as nurses, working extremely hard for appalling salaries. For the first seven years of their marriage, they lived in two rooms on the fourth floor of an old house with no bathroom or running water. How did their mental health suffer? Apparently having to use public baths to bathe, and walk four floors to use the outside toilet didn't harm their wellbeing. When, as a nation did, we get so soft? My generation and our children's generation have literally never had it so good, and yet we whine.

The shift seems to be that now instead of thinking of the big picture and counting your blessings, society has become increasingly selfish.

The luxury of too much time to think about one's self. I bring this up because I fear it has crept into the profession. Nursing has always been a vocation, placing the patient front and centre. The system now seems skewed, with the emphasis on the individual nurse. The internet is littered with nurses on long term sick or having huge issues with mental health. I go back to my training, and say if the work is not suited to you, find another job.

Even a vocational and dedicated nurse will inevitably sometimes be stressed with the demands and strain of the workload. Something every partner of a nurse knows, is that when we get out of work we vent. The trick is not being over burdened by the emotional load of your day and equally not overwhelming your family.

Spend long enough as a nurse and you become immune to gore. I recall one Sunday morning my husband called into question the fact that we were watching a training video whilst eating our fried breakfast. Putting a tube down some poor patient's throat, while simultaneously putting a great big needle through the abdomen wall to fit a feeding tube, apparently, is not good breakfast viewing. There in lies the problem, it is a fine balance bringing your work home.

My husband has been incredibly supportive these many years living with a nurse. I think there should be a booklet to inform and support our families from the very beginning. When you come out of work, raging in anger, or weeping at someone else's grief you need to let it out. If your nearest and dearest are faint of heart or stomach, talk to another nurse, no one really understands what we do but us. To stay the course and have longevity without madness, another tool is the ability to shed work and switch off at home. Keep it sharp, hone it, it is your best weapon of defence in protecting yourself. Rant if you must, get it off your chest and the nurses fail safe of a large glass of wine, but then let it go.

In my last role Fridays were brutal. 8am start could often result in 10 hours or more of relentless work. The cancer meeting was a veritable bun fight of managing the case load, making urgent calls and prepping and attending a cancer clinic. New patients were informed of their diagnosis with their families, struggling post operative patients were counselled and old patients could present with recurrence of their disease. There was very rarely time for a break, food would be taken that could be grabbed in-between patients and as I walked out of the hospital my brain was spiralling with information and the trauma of the day. We had been married for many years and as my husband collected me from outside the hospital he knew not to speak. My capacity to process chitchat was gone. Every Friday night I would walk into the safety and love of my family with a pint of tea and an extremely large glass of wine ready for me.

    It creeps up on you, and nurses vary greatly in their success but this ability to shield yourself when not at work enables you to rest and recover to fight another day. There is a strength you find, to do what is difficult and what is hard, and not damage yourself in the process. Inner grit, to hold back tears when a patient wails with grief takes practise and skill. The knowledge and determination to move a patient though you know they are in pain. Despite their protestations you must do what needs to be done, because to fail will condemn them to more complications and pain. It is knowing you have to do the obnoxious things, but always with as much tenderness, patience and kindness. No matter how much you may like or dislike your patient and how knackered you are; your patient should never be aware.

    I remember thinking when I first started working in endoscopy I had joined a torture chamber. Name an orifice and we stuck cameras in it, not one examination is a pleasant experience and all are universally dreaded by the patient. The work is surely fit for a masochist you would think, so how to manage this without being totally demoralised. My solution was to make a bad situation as comfortable as possible. A well held hand and a soothing voice can be more effective than pain relief sometimes. Fully explaining what is about to happen and talking a patient calmly through their ordeal yields positive results. So, no matter how horrid your job, how dysfunctional the team and inept the management, you go home with your head held high because you helped, and your patients were grateful. The rest is just noise.

It is always, (no matter how long you have been in the job) vital to protect yourself against bad habits. The key principle should be first and foremost patient care. Woe-be-tide anyone, no matter how senior who tries to jeopardise this. The nurse's job is to always stand up and speak out, firstly as the patient's advocate and secondly to support, and back up your colleagues. In an era where politicians and accountants dictate the running of the NHS it is glaringly obvious, they are not experts in patient care, that buck stops with you.

At the end of my nurse training the world turned. The hospital had been run very efficiently by a head nurse and a medical director, and immediately beneath them a fleet of matrons who in turn oversaw every ward. The ward sister was a formidable beast, usually scary and rarely friendly. She was not there to be your friend; she was there to run with military precision a safe and efficient ward.

In true old school tradition, the head nurse was a spinster, she was married to her job, married to the hospital. At Epsom hospital she was a small Japanese woman who glided through the corridors, her eagle eyes spotting a ladder in your tights, the wrong earrings or a rogue hair out of place at a hundred yards. As afraid of her as we all were, she commanded respect. She was omnipresent and all seeing and gave you confidence that all was as it should be. Just as I qualified it was announced she was retiring and so we began the descent on the slippery slope to privatisation.

Idiotic idea number three, let's take a successful businessman who has spent his life making money and turning a profit and put him in charge of the business whose only customers bleed the service dry. Medicine is not a business, patients do not, or should not, pay for their care that was the ethos of the NHS. The new general manager who replaced our formidable lead nurse was a very successful businessman, he had made his money in vinyl flooring (apparently). I joked that patient care would plummet, because how can you run an organisation without any understanding of the intricacies, diversities and numerous challenges that come with caring for the sick. I visited the hospital for a small reunion a year later, and, oh how we laughed, as we admired the fabulous new fancy vinyl floors in our outpatient department. Talking to those nurses still working in the hospital it was evident standards had already started to fall.

So many problems have arisen from the top-heavy management, mostly comprised of overpaid business professionals who haven't got the first clue about medicine and what should be prioritised and valued. Stop wasting valuable resources on PR and inclusion and get feet on the ground to provide basic care. Highly paid experienced nursing teams are employed for the sole purpose of worrying about inclusion. This is because managers who are not medical, treat the NHS like any other huge organisation. It is a ludicrous and unnecessary waste of money when patients are being left unfed and unwashed due to the shortage of nurses on the wards. You surely don't need to be medical to see the immorality and stupidity of this. It is not sexy, it is not rocket-science, but getting the basics right underpin everything.

Orthopaedics

With one block on a ward of female medicine under my belt, the group all gathered back at school, heaving a collective huge sigh of relief. We had all survived and most importantly no patients had been harmed at our hands. We often worked on wards in pairs, which was immensely reassuring knowing there was someone else who knew as little as you, which was a comfort.

There are no stupid questions! This has followed me my whole career. The most dangerous nurse is the one who doesn't know what they don't know, if in doubt ask. If not in doubt still ask.

I am on a national nursing group online, often nurses will ask for advice if applying for a specific position or questions about pensions or sick leave *et cetera*. One such message was from a student nurse who had just qualified and was terrified of starting her job as a staff nurse and asked for people's best advice. I read the many comments, comfortable shoes, don't panic, it's going to be hard, which in my opinion were all valid. Most offered you should keep a large selection of pens in your work bag, (I think all medical practitioners even do a module at university now on pen theft) as this has never changed in all my years. I felt moved to say, seek out the experienced nurse who wants to impart wisdom and remember there are no stupid questions.

Lots of thumb's ups and smiley emoji's then one comment I took exception to. "Of course there are stupid questions". A question may appear stupid to a person who knows the answer, but if left unasked it is the nurse giving the wrong drug dose, clamping the wrong drain or a hundred other calamitous actions. So, I say again there are no stupid questions. Worryingly there are stupid nurses.

Currently the group is haemorrhaging messages of despair, it seems every hospital is understaffed and there is a clear correlation. Not enough staff = patient care suffers. Nurses implode and are leaving in their droves. Never since Florence started it all has the nursing profession been so fragile. The decline in the profession hurts my heart. The true sadness are the endless stories of awful treatment that some patients receive as a result.

My second placement was an orthopaedic ward, and I liked it. There was something straightforward and mechanical, if it is broken, fix it. So much so when I finished my training it was the first permanent role I had as a newly qualified nurse. For all the negative reasons not to be nurse, there is one certainty and advantage in nursing, if you want a job, you can get one tomorrow. I was 22, newly married, a mortgage payer and had relocated to Staffordshire. I thought I would check out the local hospital and join their bank (a hospital agency to cover shortages of staff) to work on lots of wards to see where I wanted to land.

"Do you like orthopaedics?" One of the two nurses I had met for an informal meeting asked me.

"Yes, I suppose" harking back to my second placement three years earlier.

"Great, start Monday they need a full-timer."

So, in a matter of minutes, I had a new permanent job. How hard can it be I thought, how wrong I was.

I turned up keen on my first day to the loveliest hospital I've ever worked in. Hartshill Orthopaedic Hospital in Stoke which has long since been demolished. But then it sat high on a hill a vintage offshoot of the main general hospital. Originally built as a sanatorium, a place where patients with TB (Tuberculosis) would have spent months or possibly years. For anyone young enough not to know about these hospitals find Betty McDonald's book 'The Plague and I' for a great account of this type of hospital. It was planned like an octopus with the central building housing clinics and offices and then long wards ran out like spokes of a wheel. Rooms were either single or four bedded, all had old Crittall French doors and concrete ramps leading outside. In the days of rampant TB and before the advent of antibiotics, patients were nursed on bedrest often outside under rubber sheets. (See Photo 8)

My father who caught TB from a patient and spent two years in a sanatorium. He was allowed visitors once a week, apparently hated the man in the bed next to him – for over two years! He lost a lung and died of cancer aged 42 probably due to the twice-weekly x-rays he had for the duration of his stay. It was a terrible disease and took many lives. As a nurse my father was keen to try the new thing – antibiotics. Sadly, his old consultant didn't believe in these newfangled ideas and continued to stick an enormous needle through my dad's ribs every week to collapse the lung hoping rest would cure it. All this achieved was excruciating pain until finally his lung refused to inflate. On her visit every Sunday he would tell my mother how the new admissions on the other wards were being treated with antibiotics and escaping in a couple of weeks.

TB has largely been forgotten in this country but this ward was a reminder of darker days. The land and gardens between each ward screened it from view from its neighbour, making it an ideal configuration in the 1980's for an orthopaedic ward. Traction, bed-rest and long stays were often the case. On a nice day every bed could be pushed outside, and in those days offered many patients the opportunity to smoke.

So here I was at this delightful scene, immensely proud and delighted in my cornflower blue dress and pillbox lace hat. Three years of hard labour and you got a medal and I felt the bee's knees. My hospital badge proudly on one side of my chest, beautifully enamelled with the Thames and a horse's head, and the national badge to prove I had done it, I had qualified! They seem to have done away with them now and most nurses work in some form of theatre scrub. It is hard to be smart and proud in faded ink marked shabby scrubs.

Also, a tradition that is lost is the nurse's buckle. It was a momentous day, myself, husband, mother and in-laws spent a day in the Brighton Lanes, searching for the perfect one. I knew it the moment I saw it, silver and square it had an art deco feel comprising a row of snowdrops, I could take on the world in that getup. With a few deep breaths I walked onto the ward for the first time, the welcome and fanfare I had hoped for was disappointing to say the least.

"Sit down, I haven't got long I've got to get my kids to school." The night nurse began handover, every shift hands over to the next. Now there are electronic handover sheets that can be printed but then it relied on two things the speed and shorthand of the arriving nurse and the concise and thorough imparting of facts from the nurse going home.

My knowledge of orthopaedic terminology was minimal, and her patience wore thin.

"When will the other staff be here?" I asked mid diatribe as she reeled off patient's names I could only just catch and their diagnosis, which I was hazy on.

"It's you, Sister's sick and the auxiliaries are already washing the patients."

I managed to jot down all the names. Just when I thought she had finished my mild terror at being the only qualified nurse on the ward catapulted to a whole new level. I thought I might actually throw up.

"In the nursery."

"Nursery?" I blurted, "No one said there would be a nursery!"

"There is one baby in the nursery on traction following surgery but her mum stays with her 24/7".

I was at least thankful for the five empty cots. She looked at me, exhausted, craving her bed. She only had capacity for a sympathetic smile, patted me on the shoulder and dropped the keys on the desk.

"You'll be fine, just don't kill anyone. The girls are great they know what to do". And then she was gone.

I was the sole, singular, lone, qualified nurse on the ward. Talk about baptism by fire. I learnt to love that ward, not only the work, but the team. It was a valuable lesson that we can all learn from each other, the team of auxiliaries were so experienced and dedicated they supported and taught me so much. The work was interesting with eight consultants to juggle, each with different demands.

"No, his stitches have to come out day ten. No, it's Mr Wynn Jones, his patient's stitches have to come out on alternate days, half after nine days, and the remaining half day ten. No, no Mr Khan's patients have their stitches out at day twelve! Don't you know this yet?" The ward sister informed me week two. I always think of this time in my career when I hear the term 'steep learning curve'. Those early days felt like vertical climbing without a safety rope for comfort.

Consultants were always accompanied by the nurse in charge on ward rounds, I nodded, noted and smiled and as soon they had left the ward, I would get the 'girls', most of whom were in their 50s to interpret and set the correct form of traction that was still a blur to me.

What about the nursery? I hear you ask. There was indeed a six-cot nursery and as an orthopaedic specialist hospital they performed complex spinal surgery. Luckily in my early days it was mainly the poor babies with hip dysplasia laying on their backs with legs up in traction.

Although there was a toddler in halo traction with steel pins fixed into her skull to hang weights from, forming a metal halo around her head. The head traction and straps on the legs pulling the other way rendered her immobile. Not dissimilar to a mediaeval torture device anyone who has had a toddler can image how frustrated and unhappy she was. I didn't enjoy her being there, although it was undoubtedly much worse for her and her poor family.

I was a fervent advocate for open visiting so nearly always a parent or grandparent was there. In my twenties I had no experience or desire to have anything to do with children – especially in a professional capacity, and was delighted to never have a major issue in the nursery whilst I working there.

Welcome idiotic idea number four, why did we change the name of auxiliaries and why did we go from one word to four? I still don't understand. Now called Health Care Support Workers, HCSW. I suspect it was a reaction to increasing the jobs the NHS have asked them to do. Student nurses used to be the backbone of care on the wards. Every shift would have a selection of first, second- and third-year student nurses all vying to complete the daily tasks, to tick off the long list of practical skills that needed to be honed and perfected. Practice makes perfect and not content to catheterise a hand full of patients in your student days as they do now, we aimed to have done dozens if not hundreds by the time we qualified.

Student nurses now may well be working in Costa or Tesco whilst doing their degree to pay for it, it has left a void. So, the auxiliary was rebranded and the raft of procedures and care fell on their shoulders. With no formal training and certainly no pay increases the hardest working members of the team now take the burden of nearly all the hands-on care on a ward.

Of course, some are exceptional and work well above their pay grade, but is this fair? Traditionally there were two levels of nurse, a state enrolled nurse and a state registered nurse. The enrolled nurse training was shorter and more practical but it was still two years of intensive training. We now ask our HCSW's to do the work of enrolled nurses with no professional body, union protection or standard framework and training. Fundamentally they are working as nurses, but

being paid as auxiliaries. Yet again we have reinvented the wheel with no real benefit.
It is yet another loss for the nursing profession as qualified nurses spend more time on computers than caring for their patients.

There is still a glass ceiling and although HCSW's can now achieve a pay band four (Newly qualified nurses start at band 5) and work as highly specialised members of the team they are not nurses but endure the stress and strain of a difficult job. They can be integral to a team and work at a level commensurate to their nursing colleagues but will never have the professional and financial security and rewards.

I should talk here about moving to another trust or hospital, it is tough! All you know changes, procedures are different, nearly all charts and documentation are designed by the hospital itself. One hospital's stool chart is pink, then you move to your new job and now it's blue. It may seem a minor change but to be efficient and safe you have to have a full understanding of all things. I'm sure today's nurses will be faced with a myriad of different computer programmes that dictate their daily lives. Each hospital will decide which computerised system to purchase and may vary significantly to a neighbouring hospital. It invariably has zero benefit for the patient but keeps the auditors busy and computer techs rich. It's just a matter of getting used to new things but you do learn, to learn fast. Not only was this delightful hospital antiquated but so too were some of its practices.

  One old Hartshill treatment which I have never seen used elsewhere, and I'm sure is obsolete now, was the lovely 'twilight therapy'. Before the similarly named vampire books, this was used to treat chronic bad backs. Patients would be admitted on Friday with deformed curved spines and painful shuffling gaits. Thankful for any medical professional to hear their story, it had often been months if not years of chronic pain leading to this admission. As soon as their story was taken, they were placed on a bed and legs, from groin to ankle shaved. Elastoplast tape would be secured from the hip down under the foot and up the inner thigh. With the aid of bandages, string and extremely heavy weights and pulleys, traction would be applied to both legs. The bed would have to be tilted with the head as far down as possible to counterbalance the pull on the legs. These were the easiest patients to care for, because part of the treatment was a concoction of sedatives, muscle relaxants and extremely strong painkillers. And so began their 48 hours of twilight therapy.

They were without doubt the most compliant and undemanding patients I have ever cared for. Drifting in and out of stupor they rarely ate and existed on what ever fluid you could encourage them to drink with the straw. There was no leaving this position for the whole weekend and they willingly laid and were bed bathed and all other needs taken care of with a bed pan.

I had no understanding of the theory or rationale for this treatment but inevitably on Monday patients walked, (staggered) home in less pain and better posture than when they had arrived. For the staff it made for a nice quiet shift at work.

Preparing someone for surgery involved admission the day before and then a pink scrub, kill-all solution was used in a long hot shower the night before, and on the morning of their operation. There was always an abundance of shaving, 'nipple to knee' was the theory back then, a job I really enjoyed. A cheap razor and plenty of suds was a great way to pass a late shift.

It is and was standard practice in all hospitals to have a checklist to prepare your patient, jewellery free, in a hospital gown *et cetera*. But they were thorough up north and every patient had paper knickers, a paper hat, paper socks and quite bizarrely a brown luggage label tied around their ankle or toe stating their name and proposed surgery. I found this all a little strange but like any good nurse you do as you are told. What I hadn't bargained on was the screaming theatre Sister spitting in my face as she informed me in no uncertain terms of my error.

"What do you mean, you didn't order the milk float for his blood's!" I'm sure that statement makes as much sense to you as it did to me on that day. Apparently as a stand-alone building, essential supplies had to be requested and transported on a milk float from the main hospital. It was a novel yet effective system and always made me smile when a patient went trundling off to the main site laid in the back of a milk float. Apparently, I had to pre-order the patients blood transfusion should he need it during surgery. That was my only faux pas and that theatre nurse never forgot and never smiled at me again, but equally I never forgot to book my bloods.

There were so many things to learn, not only the facts like where are the organs, what do they do, and why do they go wrong. Added to this the myriad of procedures and protocols that you learn along the way. But there are also subtleties and skills in how to care. To be a patient is to be vulnerable, there will be pain, there will be frustration and there inevitably will be fear. Any nurse can dish out medicines and do dressings, but a good nurse uses every minute with a patient to assess the whole.

Whether on an orthopaedic ward, or in any interaction with a patient the real skill comes in multitasking. You may appear to be, by an onlooker, to merely be taking away a dinner tray, but in that moment you have assessed your patient. How is their mood, are they happy? If not why not? Are they comfortable? Are they struggling to move, are they warm enough? Why haven't they got Anti embolism stockings (pressure socks to prevent blood clots in the legs) on? Are they drinking enough? Why is the tea not touched and the jug still full? Did they eat? Could they not manage, should they have had help? A quick look at drains and catheters, do they need emptying? Are they dehydrated? Do they have a fever? Observe and document. Ask and assist always.

Collecting breakfast trays give you an early indication of all the patients and who needs your help first. A really thorough way to plan your shift. If you work a late shift in the afternoon or a night shift, walk around and say hello.

"Hello, my name is Anne and I'm going to be looking after you this evening." It certainly isn't difficult but it's enormously powerful. You will immediately set your patient at ease (Or give them good warning if you are substandard) There is never a wasted interaction, the moment you tidy a table may be the moment that that patient decides to admit a fear that has deprived them of sleep.

Always look your patients in the eye and ask;

"How are you?"

This sound too simple to mention but hospitals have launched expensive and elaborate schemes to reinforce things that should come naturally to any well trained, good nurse. Sadly, and I can hear the people slating me now, now everyone is striving that nurses have degrees and masters and specialist courses. We have developed a generation with a 'too posh to wash mentality'. Without the basics, we are lost.

I recently took a friend to an 'Acute Oncology Assessment' ward. Having cancer and mid chemotherapy infections must be dealt with swiftly. Imagine my confusion and dismay when I asked three qualified nurses, all sat chatting in an office if they could assess my friends pressure areas, as she was developing sores.

"We don't really keep dressings on the ward, and the tissue viability nurse Specialist only works Thursday".

The apathy was enough to make me want to swear. Keeping composure, I asked politely if they were in fact qualified nurses. I suggested they could take the internal stairs to a surgical ward where I was confident the nurse in charge would have given them some dressings. It absolutely beggars believe that this is what we have come to. When I collected my friend, I found a dry gauze had been placed on her sore which we had to soak off at home and I ordered some dressing from the internet.

The biggest tool on the nurse's Swiss army knife is communication. Used correctly it can soothe the fearful, diffuse the angry and encourage the hopeless.

The incident that stays with me as a junior nurse working on an orthopaedic ward on night duty was the consummate example of this. Handover should always be conducted behind closed doors and can be brutal.

"Mrs Q in bed 13 is a complete and utter pain in the arse!"

It was one such preamble to the 11-hour night shift that the day nurse was ranting about the stuck-up bitch in the side room. There was murmuring agreement but as I'd never met her, I made it my goal to have her happy and liking me by morning.

She had suffered a catastrophic car crash. I can't divulge all the details but the man she was with either died or was badly injured. Randomly I do remember it was a Porsche. She was transferred from intensive care to the ward I was working on. Her stomach that had ruptured in the crash, I clearly remember she had just had a pub lunch that included white wine, chicken and sweetcorn; apparently it was all swilling around her abdomen. The surgeon spent ages retrieving free-roaming sweetcorn from around her organs.

She also had a head injury, broken arm, broken leg in a plaster and a fractured pelvis. To the day staff she'd been a complete pain,

"Does she think she's a private patient, I wish I could take her bell off her," one moaned.

As soon as the day shift leave the qualified nurse does the drugs round and student nurses and auxiliaries start the process of bedding down or settling everyone for the night. You check the fluid in and out, whizz around, with hopefully the last bedpan and helping patients to bed. I volunteered to do 'the problem patient' or 'buzzer queen' as she was also known. There she lay, totally unable to reposition herself and could do nothing unaided. She was sweating and uncomfortable and obviously her nerves were shredded. She was abrupt, she was bossy, she was downright rude but fundamentally she was afraid, in pain and grieving.

Firstly, I acknowledged her plight, often that is all a patient needs; to know you understand, you believe them. Then I struck a bargain. If she would not buzz, as soon as everyone else was settled I would come in and give her a bed bath and clean sheets and try my best to make her comfortable. We worked a pattern of seven nights in a row that's 77 hours a week. The reward was five days off; but it was still a zombie inducing grind. But that week the nights flew by and our routine developed. I would give her a top to toe wash even at 2 am, one night dragging in the tray and bucket to wash her hair for the first time since the accident weeks before. She was a prisoner in that single room with unimaginable physical pain and trying to come terms with such a life altering accident. Remember this was a time before mobile phones, tablets, kindles or TVs in hospital rooms. All she had to distract her was a magnolia ceiling and the view of a patch of sky. She was prisoner and totally dependent on her carers.

She was a kind and intelligent woman and needed care commensurate to her physical and psychological injuries. I still have her letters of thanks, but I thank her for teaching me to see through someone's behaviour as it is just a symptom of their struggle.

I have spent the rest of my career stepping up to difficult cases, dealing with the patients that others don't want to deal with. The challenge is winning over a patient who hates everyone, and this can be one of the most rewarding things you do.

Orthopaedics truly is the repair shop of medicine, there is something hugely gratifying in admitting a patient who is broken, fixing them and sending them home happy. It really showed me the resilience of people's character and often a determination, even against great odds. One case which was huge proof of this was when a frail lady in her eighties who stumbled and fell beneath a lorry, three lots of double wheels ran over her legs and she sustained appalling injuries. When I first encountered her, I remember thinking I would rather have been killed than have to face a future of imminent agony and long-term disability, especially at her age.

One of her legs had been completely amputated close to her pelvis, she sustained numerous pelvic fractures and any movement was excruciating for her. The pelvis took weeks, into months to repair as she lay on the bed. Her remaining leg was a patchwork of lumpy flesh held together with hundreds of clips. The nearest thing to Frankenstein's monster I have ever seen in the flesh.

Her x-rays were something to behold fragments of bone precariously pieced together with plates and screws and only time would tell if it would all knit and join together to give her a functioning leg. Apart from obvious pain every time you had to move her, she was consistently uncomplaining. She exceeded all expectations and over the many weeks her injuries repaired. I always had a sense of dread when I pulled back the sheets, as it baffled me that so much damage was recoverable. Always positive and reassuring to her face, I constantly doubted the leg would survive its ordeal. One of my favourite jobs as a nurse is removing stitches and clips, it's like peeling wallpaper only more satisfying. I claimed the role of clip remover and spaced it out over three days, first taking every third, then the next day alternate until the hundreds of clips were out.

That lady was a lesson to me not to give up hope, as recovery from even the most awful injuries is achievable. Not only did she learn to hop on her remaining leg but could transfer into a wheelchair. Months after being admitted, self-propelled herself from the ward to go home. Maybe giving birth half a dozen times, outliving two husbands and surviving the war gives you the strength to recover from being run over by juggernaut.

It is often the old, life experienced patients who impress you by their courage and determination. More recently I had a patient of twenty who squirmed and complained of being needle phobic when I tried to take blood. She had a stunning array of piercings and was covered in numerous tattoos. I admit on this occasion my level of compassion was unusually very low, and my sympathy, for her, was virtually non-existent. Uncaring you may say, but true. She saw nothing but my usual professional front but inside I was screaming, 'suck it up, for goodness sake'.

In a speciality that routinely repairs people and sends them home fixed, it is often harder to deal with the failures. Cases where surgery isn't an option and where the team and the patient must face the sad truth that they cannot be mended.

The patient that will always stay with me and epitomises this was flown to us from Africa. A valued employee of an oil company, he had broken his back. Determined to give him the best treatment he had been flown to the little hospital in Staffordshire. In their best efforts to preserve his spine and protect his spinal column he had been placed in a plaster bed, a low wooden tray in which he lay completely surrounded by plaster. The smell was something I won't ever forget, as his time in this tray it had acted as his bedpan. He was very quickly taken to the operating theatres and chipped out of his wrappings, unfortunately although the fractures were secured the damage to his spinal cord was obviously not recoverable. This poor man who spoke not one word of English laid in a cubicle for many weeks with no visitors, and no family for support. I think back now and wonder why an interpreter was not found or anyone who could communicate for him.

But there he lay, our only communication smiles and nods as everyday we washed him and more importantly, tended the most terrific pressure sores I'd ever seen. In an effort to save his spine the team in Africa had condemned him to a pressure sore on his sacrum, (the bottom of the back above and between the buttocks) that I could fit my fist into. He also had huge sores on both heels and shoulder blades which luckily healed quite quickly. The only upside of being paralysed was he felt no pain and every other day I would dress his wounds.

His flesh had gone down to his bones, and the hideousness of it was equalled only by the satisfaction of seeing it heal. I decorated his room for Christmas even buying him a little tree; not knowing what his religion was, or whether he even celebrated Christmas but I thought my guide would be his reaction, and if he smiled it could stay. His huge smile was all the answer and thanks I needed.

I left the ward before he was discharged and I have wondered over the years what became of him, did he ever get home to his family in Africa? I know with certainty, sadly, that he would never walk again.

Although this is all sounding rather bleak, in actuality orthopaedics is a relatively fun place to be. Often apart from their breaks and surgeries, if well controlled with pain relief most patients do not in themselves feel unwell. And the, camaraderie and banter on the wards made for an enjoyable place to be.

It was a joyous day indeed when the owner of the local Thai restaurant fell from the third-floor window and broke her neck. Obviously not a good day for her, but there were definitely two benefits for me. I knew the theory of the Stryker bed but had never used one, but because of her unstable neck fractures it was a necessity. It is a cross between a flower press and a sandwich toaster. There is a gap for the face on one surface and strategically placed holes for the bottom. Like roasting on a spit, you could turn the large handle at the bottom of the bed and spin the patient through 180°. Sandwiched between the two mattresses and secured with huge butterfly bolts she could be laid on her front and her book positioned under her to change position and enable her to read.

Being completely flat for weeks on end does not give you an appetite and try as they might her staff would bring her in numerous tempting little dishes in takeaway containers. Despite our encouragement she had no desire to eat and rather conveniently the 6 o'clock drug round would coincide with her often saying,

"Just take it away I don't want it".

This became the second benefit for me, so began the routine of small delicious Thai meals at the end of the drug round. Strangely never in my career have I been more willing to work the late shift, and never since have tasted such good Thai food. You will be glad to hear she recovered well and walked out with a neck brace weeks later.

I only worked at Hartshill for just over a year as by husband's job relocated us back down to Kent. I remember crying for a good couple of days when I left, it truly was a lovely place to work. But this was back in the late 80s and no one left a job without a proper send-off. I had seen it as a student nurse at Epsom, colleagues who were leaving would be dropped in a bath of water, but they really didn't do things by half in Staffordshire.

It was my last day, and I had done the drugs and was due to leave in a few hours. There had been lots of giggling and I guessed something was afoot. Then just before lunch I was accosted by a group of my colleagues and dragged into one of the large bathrooms. The bath was full to the brim with copious amounts of pink cleaning solution, baked beans, bacon rind, a few kippers floating amongst the cornflakes and anything else they could scrape from the breakfast trays. They had the decency to let me remove my buckle and watch then fully clothed, I was dropped in the bath.

Much hilarity was had by all, including all the able-bodied patients who could watch from the corridor. A colleague, I misguidedly thought of as a friend, offered to retrieve my clothes from the locker room so I handed over my key and tried to extricate myself from the slimy lumpy bath. Once in the staffroom I stripped off, crying with the raw emotion of having to say goodbye whilst laughing as I picked baked beans from my hair. A knock at the door and more raucous laughter as a pile of hospital clothing was handed to me. The pink hospital nightdress with the obligatory split up the back, a dressing gown finished off with the paper hat, knickers, and slippers that our patients wore.

Tied to my ankle a patient identification label (See back cover)

In the day room staff from adjoining wards, doctors and patients said their goodbyes whilst I sat on a commode with my paper bedpan hat, adorned with hanging tampons. Although my shift was far from over my ability to work had long gone and I welcomed the wine they handed me. Just to be clear before there were cries of having me struck off, another nurse was in charge and quite sober.

By this time, I was a sobbing wreck and had no defences to prevent them bandaging me to the arms of the commode and pushing me out onto the high street. I couldn't have cared less, so bereft was I at having to leave. Today I'm sure everyone would be punished and dragged over the coals for unprofessional behaviour but to me it showed I would be missed and I had been appreciated. I was pushed safely back into the hospital by a bus driver, given my clothes to change into, and driven home.

I continued to work in orthopaedics when I relocated to Tunbridge Wells. Sadly, the trauma ward often felt like a waiting room for God, and was allocated a relentless stream of sad elderly people usually with broken hips, who rarely fared well and often died. It was not now the speciality I had loved and I was soon looking to move on.

See How You Like It

From stories of my parent's days training to be nurses in the 50s, to life as a student nurse in the 80s, it appears that much had changed. They told of intricate procedures and practices they would test out on each other. One day as students they had to do a complex skullcap bandage - capable of retaining its shape when lifted off. Apparently, my father and his friend were messing around and bandaged my father's ears down and out. I guess I inherit my hysterical laughter from my mum and she had an attack of it in the classroom. But those really were the good old days and matron took her outside and threw a bucket of cold water all over her.

Modern day nurses will never know the frustration of smashing a glass thermometer. In my day it was merely a matter of gathering up the Mercury on paper hand towels and throwing it down the plug hole or in the bin (I know health and safety would have fit now) but in my parents' day you would be marched to the matron's office and the cost of the equipment taken from your salary. Things certainly had changed.

My parents practised passing nasogastric tubes, up the nose and down to the stomach on each other in the classroom, they shaved and injected each other. By the 80s we were somewhat more mambi pambi and drew the line at such things. There were still some old school consultants and nurses that inflicted such pain on us though.

We were in school studying diabetes and the endocrine system and a grey haired, humourless consultant took our class. Slowly he walked around our tables placing a 1ml syringe, a glass ampoule of water and a tissue in front of each one of us. We smirked and smiled; we were experts. Didn't he know we had injected numerous peaches? With a large cough he stood at the front of the class, his demeanour and mere presence dictated silence and we all looked keenly up at him. Very slowly he talked us through the role of insulin, types of diabetes and its treatments. Confidently we all drew up water into our syringes as instructed- what none of us were ready for were his next three words.

"Expose your abdomen" Hesitantly, very reluctantly in some cases shirts were lifted. "Pinch with the non-dominant hand," again with shaking hands and fearful darting looks between us all we did as we were told. "Press the needle into your abdomen, firmly and slowly then depress the plunger."

He showed no emotion, he looked like he would not accept non-compliance so with a small chorus of ouches we all injected ourselves. In retrospect it was a testament to the strength of his demeanour that a class full of young girls blindly followed orders.

Do student nurses still do this? I very much doubt it, but it served a valuable lesson that injecting yourself is far harder than injecting someone else. On the wards today we don't blink at sending patients home with a bag of needles to inject themselves with anticlotting drugs. If you have never done it to yourself, how can you truly appreciate the need to explain it clearly and most importantly, understand the fear and trepidation of your patients.

We also spent a whole day blindfolded taking it in turns to guide your buddy for the day. Without this exercise I would never have the depth of appreciation for the hazards and issues visually impaired people face - smacking your legs into furniture focuses one's mind.

If you are thinking of becoming a nurse, or just for the fun of it, do brush someone else's teeth and have them brush yours. For the sake of all patients, I hope university still does make nurses practice on each other before letting them loose on patients.

The cape is another part of our uniform to be relegated to history, they were thick and they were warm and incredibly quick to don when leaving the ward. I had one and my parents had them, but they are no more. What every nurse still needs like every good superhero is a shield or cape. It protects you from your patients, whether it is their anger, grief or pain. Conversely it protects the patient from your fear, embarrassment or inexperience. No patient wants to know it's the first time you've done a procedure, don your cape of confidence and don't let them see your fear. It is one of the most crucial items in a nurse's toolkit.

When you start out with a fresh face, good knees and an unsullied spine (all doomed to be buggered if you continue in the profession) the wards are rife with challenges. Embarrassment is usually the first, even six weeks in school didn't prepare you for the first time you wash a man's genitals. My advice would be to start old, if possible, with a man whose marbles may be less than intact. Rule number one is, if at all possible, get the patient to wash their own intimate areas. You can soap the cloth, rinse it out and hand the towel. Sometimes, and here is the crucial point, if the patient can't, you must! This is not open to interpretation; it is your job. A male medical ward or better still, a care of the elderly ward will soon shed your inhibitions, rid you of the delicacies. Pretty soon you'll have catheters gleaming and pubic areas fresh, sweet smelling, and more importantly comfortable and infection free.

    I believe I was on the first ward of my second year, I was riding high flaunting the second strip on my hat when I encountered the most embarrassing situation ever. I was a dab hand at the vacuum drains, could catheterise people with aplomb and confidently showed first-year students how to remove wound drains and sutures. Probably the qualified nurses could see the confidence I exuded and thought it was time I was put in my place.

    Sitting tall in my bright new hat I dutifully noted all the patients on my small notepad during handover. Name, age, diagnosis, surgery date and any issues to be aware of, now having a firm handle the abbreviations. Instead of having to write catheter bag draining, CBD made it clear. Similarly, IVI for intra-venous infusion and WD for wound drain, so on, and so on. Every speciality will have their own abbreviations. ERCP stands for 'Endoscopic Retrograde Cholangio Pancreatography', which is not to be confused with ERPC which is in fact 'Evacuation of Retained Products of Conception'. It is all too easy to get your gallstones and miscarriages confused. Learning the abbreviations on a new ward is a priority and I felt confident I'd got it sussed.

The ward was male Urology. TURP (Trans Urethral Resection of Prostate) I knew and understood. When the handover nurse stated with a smirk to the nurse in charge, 'PP every 15 minutes' I hesitated as I wrote it in my book. I was sure we hadn't covered this in school, and as hard as I thought I could only come to one conclusion, and prayed I wasn't allocated this patient. Over and over, for the rest of the handover my quiet mantra was, not 14, not room 14, please not room 14. I would take the confused diabetic in the side room who tries to pinch your bottom but please God not room 14.

The early shift departed and the evening's work was allocated.

"Anne room 12 to 18."

And there it was. Step one was to quietly ask the nurse in charge exactly what that meant.

"That's right bed 2 room 14 you did hear correctly PP, penile pulses every 15 minutes."

It was without doubt the longest shift of my career. The poor man in question was in his 50s. Above the sheets he looked like one of my friends' fathers, none of whom I had ever thought of in a sexual way. Growing up in a household of one parent who never dated I was spared the cringe-making realisation that old people had sex! He had been admitted with priapism - the unfortunate condition of an erection that won't go away. He had been injected in the base of his penis in order to achieve an erection, unfortunately for him, and me, it had worked too well. But now here we were, a six bedded room with five rowdy fellow patients coping the best way possible with humour at his plight and at my expense. Every 15 minutes I would walk into the room as inconspicuously as possible, hoping against hope that the joke had worn thin but until 9pm that evening every 15 minutes I would pull the curtains to calls of:

"Stand by your bed's lads, it's cock watch."

"It will never go down love, with you keep fiddling with it."

I would try to smile professionally as I pulled back the covers from the bed cradle across his middle protecting his poor engorged penis and a little of his pride. Because of the risk of lack of circulation and a real risk of his losing said penis, it was vital to ensure a pulse could be felt. I would feel around as discreetly as I could. As embarrassed as I was I could only begin to imagine how that poor man felt and thankfully as the evening progressed it subsided along with my blushes.

I have never nursed another priapism and, not surprisingly I have never applied for a job in urology, go figure.

Whether it is just through habit and the fact that things become less embarrassing the more you do them, embarrassing situations lessen the longer you do the job. The key is always to remember that for the patient the situations are often new to them and their embarrassment should never be discounted. It is much easier for the patient when you have perfected a calm professionalism without blushing, it just takes practice.

The handover to a new shift was always my cloak of protection. Tell me the patient is diabetic, incontinent, aggressive and immobile and I can mentally prepare. A deep breath, a girding of loins and I can approach a patient knowing what is needed. I think this is why I hated my time Casualty.

It was called Casualty then, (like the TV show), a few decades ago it was Accident and Emergency, A&E. Now we've gone all American and it's the Emergency Department ED. Why on earth departments need rebranding when they continue to offer precisely the same service, we will call idiotic idea number five.

My last hospital had an Intensive Therapy Unit, ITU. When I first started out it was ICU, Intensive Care Unit and remained so in every hospital I had worked at. At a time, unknown to me they opted to change the middle letter. Some staff still persist in calling it ITU whilst others ICU. It's a small thing but none the less an annoying one without an obvious reason.

Likewise, there was always Coronary Care Unit, CCU. Again, like every cardiac centre in the NHS this department cared for the very poorly heart patients. For some bizarre logic, that was never explained, my last hospital changed ITUs name to Critical Care Unit CCU. It beggars belief, and I never found out what the heart unit was now called so continue to call ITU, ITU. It would be so much more straightforward if the NHS managers followed the old adage, 'If it ain't broke, don't fix it!'

Back to A&E, (my preferred name as we had it for 20+ years) I have found a lot of staff who work in A&E are from the gung-ho school of medicine. They thrive on adrenaline, getting their kicks from never knowing what will come through the door next. Good for you I say, and I applaud them all, and thank goodness they exist. For me, as a nervous second year it was a place of utter terror. It was split into two distinct areas, minors and majors. Minors were trips, cuts and involved maybe an x-ray, some sympathy and dressings. Patients could normally walk, or hobble through the department and this was much my preferred environment. The patients would wait in a room and take a number and I enjoyed the challenge of getting them seen, patched up and sent on their way.

Complacency should always be challenged in nursing and on this day as I calmly marched into the waiting room to call my next number. I could easily have missed the middle-age man slumped in the corner. You must always have your wits about you and observe a room. This man was the same colour as the off-white walls, it was clear he was a workman as his clothes were covered in grime and smudges of paint. His pallor however was concerning, so forgetting the person I had gone to fetch I walked over. On close examination he was sweaty and cold to the touch, I scanned him for obvious injury but apart from some blood spots on his trousers he sat clutching a packet of salt and vinegar crisps and a hand towel. (It seems very stressful, significant experiences leave indelible memories).

"Are you okay? What seems to be the problem?" I asked and he looked slowly up at me, there were no words, but he handed me the crisp packet. Nodding and gesturing to his lap, he obviously wanted me to have it so I took it. The hand that was hidden by the bag was wrapped in the towel sodden with a dark red patch. Warily I opened the crisp bag and there covered in small crumbs and salt was his index finger. This was probably the nearest I have ever come to vomiting on a patient, but closing the bag I walked calmly to the door and not so calmly screamed.

"I need help here NOW!"

Student nurses were the cannon fodder, the workhorses of the NHS. Now they spend most of their three years in university or their second job. But back then the sea of pale blue was to be used and abused. The more junior, the more unfair the treatment, weekends off were a luxury Week long stints of night shifts and of course working every bank holiday so the senior nurses could be off having a life. If I had my way now it would be exactly the same. We learnt by grafting and repetition, something I don't believe can be replaced by lecture theatres or self-directed learning. Come on down idiotic idea number 6. As a consequence of moving learning to the university the in-house workers were removed. Student nurses no longer populate the wards for the majority of their training. So much practical learning is lost and so much quality care missed. It's undoubtedly bad for the student and tragic for the patient in the short and long term.

Linked obviously to idiotic idea number one, the following two examples I'm afraid highlight the consequence of this stupid idea and that modern trained nurses don't appreciate what they have lost.

In recent years a student informed me that they didn't miss out on practical experience as once they had qualified, that was when the learning really took place. What an astonishing waste of three years and 27 grand I would say. She further explained that once she had her degree she would specialise and learn in that area. I pitied her naivety that she would have a free moment to do anything other than cope with her days work. There is nothing as dangerous as not knowing what you don't know.

My argument is that if you specialise in Cardiology and spend a couple of years gaining a huge understanding of everything that literally makes us all tick, well that's great. Patients unfortunately come with a whole host of baggage. Caring for them not only involves specialist knowledge but a huge broad ranging understanding to deal with their prostate cancer, kidney failure, diabetes, chronic lung disease etc etc.

I don't want my mechanic to be an expert on carburettors I expect him to know enough about everything to service my car.

I frequent an online nurse forum and recently a student nurse bemoaned having to work 50 hours on a placement doing nothing but basic care that a HCSW could do and not being paid for it. Whilst I have huge sympathy and am in total agreeance that she should be paid and not have to pay for the privilege to train to be a nurse, it equally hurt my heart.

Have student nurses become so removed from caring that they don't appreciate that caring is the whole point of the exercise. It underpins every action; it informs every decision. When you attend to a patient whether it is to make the bed or help them on a bed pan your mind should be processing a myriad of information.

Walking to the end of a surgical patient's bed these are some of the thoughts that should be bouncing around your mind. For any nurse reading this you could probably think of a few things I have missed. To those not medically trained it may be a revelation that all this is whizzing around behind the smiling face of the nurse in front of you. Below is a brief list of what should be running through the nurses' mind at every encounter with a patient. This should be second nature and when you specialise add to this list twenty other considerations.

Have they got their anti-embolism stockings on to prevent clots? Are they having their daily injections for this, has anyone informed and taught the patient how to do this to themselves as they will need to on discharge?

Can they get these virtually impossible socks on and off independently? If not has anyone offered to help since their admission, and who will help them at home?

When did they last shower? Can they do this unassisted, if not what help is needed and again how will they manage at home?

How long since the surgery? Are there wound drains, staples or dissolving stitches? Always sneak a quick peek and if in doubt change the dressings.

Are they pale? What was the post operative bloods like? Check the observations for pulse and blood pressure and look up those results. Look into the lowered bottom eye lid to give you a heads up for being anaemic.

How long since they opened their bowels? Painkillers and reduced mobility and surgery will all constipate so make sure this isn't as issue or inform doctors if it is, so appropriate drugs can be prescribed.

How is the pain? Is it restricting how they move and their ability to take a deep breath which may result in a chest infection.

Ask them a question, a subtle way to see if breathing is laboured and an effort.

What are they eating and drinking? A gentle touch of the back of the hand and a soft pinch of the skin will tell you if they are dehydrated.

Are they warm enough and have all they need within reach?

Can they safely move about and have free access to their possessions and the toilet?

Who is at home for them and when are they expecting to leave, most importantly how will they manage and are there concerns that need addressing?

Has the surgery and hospital stay distressed them and are there any questions, concerns or worries you need to be aware of?

"Hello my name is Anne and I am going to be looking after you today. Any worries or anything I can help you with?"

Within two minutes or less you have assessed all the above. Don't tell me wards are too busy for this. A moment of calm eye contact whilst simultaneously gathering all the information you need to plan their care. To the student s who think washing and toileting patients is beneath them this is what it is all about. You should be spending these precious moments honing your detective skills, practising your verbal and non-verbal communication skills and learning to be a good nurse.

That fateful festive period working in A&E. I had a late shift until nine pm on Christmas Eve, and an early shift - seven thirty till four on Christmas day and of course an early on Boxing Day. And, as it was Christmas, I was allowed a day off for good behaviour before starting seven-night shifts. Yes, it was tough but it certainly makes you appreciate your time off.

I have always been a glass half full kind of gal, so hoped Christmas Day would be fun. I was young, I was naïve. I could never have anticipated how tired, harassed and angry mothers could morph into evil personified, having found themselves in

A&E on Christmas morning, (through no fault of mine I might add!). All manner of trips, falls, burns and cuts warranted them being there. Accompanied by the sourest of attitudes, they constantly informing the staff they had to get home or Christmas was ruined, and what's more, it was your fault. They oozed vitriol out of every pore, their funny Christmas pinnies and Christmas jumpers made for an odd juxtaposition. In the same vein that a clown was designed to make us laugh, but has now become the front man for terror.

"You have one and a half hours to stitch me up before my turkey is ruined!" One woman spat at me, with her hand knitted snowman jumper on, subtly splattered in blood. The padded carrot nose smiling up at me as she waved the blood-soaked festive tea towel in my face. In fact, it was the most miserable day I spent in A&E. Everyone begrudged being there, staff and patients alike. It was devoid of Christmas spirit and human kindness. So, it was with a renewed sense of doom I started the night shift on New Year's Eve.

I was lulled into a false sense of security as cheery policemen dropped in for a cup of tea and a smattering of patients. As well as the usual suspects, a good helping of middle-aged men, the years of overindulgence catching up with them with one works do too many. Now presented with heart attacks and burst ulcers. But then came the witching hours; when most decent people were safely toasting the New Year and shuffling off to bed as soon as Auld Lang Syne had finished. In A&E between twelve and three came a steady stream of drunks and the disorderly.

Princess Leia, her side bun drooping, who had taken an overdose and vomited all over her boyfriend the pirate. With an excess of alcohol and wielding a plastic cutlass, he continued to shout and wave his weapon.

"Just let her be, she'll be fine, it was a mistake." The seedy side of life and people at their most appalling is evident in the early hours.

But you adapt and you cope, and having a little dark humour goes a long way. I sympathised with the angst of the grandparents who paced around the bucket waiting for their toddler grandson to throw up. If they had known for a second, had any inkling that he would have eaten the blue loo tablet suspended in their toilet they obviously would have removed it. The boy was completely unimpressed and continued to play with his tractor. Like Violet Beauregard in Willy Wonka, he had a hew of blue about him, especially the whites of his eyes and mouth. This gave the staff endless entertainment, all of whom found an excuse to go into his room on a made-up mission to retrieve something from the cupboard. Anything for some little light entertainment. Once there was the go-ahead to give him epicak (Ipecacuanha is a plant used to make you vomit), no-one else wanted to sit in the room as he sat on the floor crying and vomiting into his bucket.

One incident that happened whilst I was not on duty was a desperately sad case. A very smart man in a three-piece suit walked in, held open his leather brief case and presented to the poor receptionists his dismembered penis. Apparently, he had been denied gender reassignment surgery so took matters into his own hands, quite literally. It goes to show how much society has changed and how desperate people can become. I believe apart from nearly bleeding to death he recovered, and she is hopefully still pottering around somewhere.

The weekends always saw a flurry of horse inflicted (it was Epsom after all) or sports injuries. Watching a rugby player have his cauliflower ear stitched back on to his head was notable for his utter bravery (although some may say stupidity). I had never particularly liked horses and certainly saw far too many kick and fall injuries to change my view.

It is local legend and quite amazing the abundance of things people managed to get stuck inside themselves. It belies belief that the story they tell is believed by anyone. Medical professionals are just that, professional to your face at least. No one will openly comment, ridicule or judge why, or how you come to have an orange stuck up your bottom but believe me nobody fell for your lame excuses.

"I was locked out and climbed through the bathroom window and fell on the orange."

No one will ask why you were locked out naked, or why was there an orange balanced conveniently on top of your toilet seat. We are all reasonably intelligent people so go with the truth, although explanations like this do give us more to laugh about later.

Without doubt the most harrowing incident was on a foggy day when the 'bat phone' rang. It was an old plug-in red phone reserved for major incidents. I always gave it a wide berth in the central office and when it rang all the staff jumped.

There had been a major incident on the M 25, the only information we had was that a coach had ploughed through the central reservation and there had been a head-on collision with the oncoming fast lane. It was early evening and we all looked out of the windows and couldn't see the cars and buildings outside due to the thick fog. We all frequented the M25, so no one was optimistic. There were drills and procedures for major incidents, which no one ever wanted to enact, but that day we did.

Being one of the most junior and least useful I was sent to the basement. Accompanying me was one of the many Maltese porters, between his language limitations and my panic it was a wonder we found what we had been sent for. Two old wicker laundry baskets the size of small sofas were pulled, pushed and dragged into the lift. Our instructions had been clear, empty the main outpatient department, and prepare for many casualties. I banged on doors, told doctors they had to leave and ushered confused patients out of the department. All the chairs were pushed aside so a triage area could be established. Following the instructions inside the baskets, a canvas capable of having poles inserted along openings each length of it were laid in rows. Wristbands, airway equipment, necessary equipment to insert drips and bags of saline were put at by each canvas, slowly filling the available floor space.

Recently watching the Nightingale temporary hospitals for Covid patients on the news bought back the terror. Remembering the fear, anticipation and the silence, and straining for the sounds of the sirens.

The porter and I paced, rearranged, waited. The A&E staff had, I'm quite sure forgotten we were there and it was a good while before we were told to stand down. Miraculously the coach driver and a man alone in his car had had a head-on collision. Both had died at the scene but no one else was injured. Mercifully the coach had been empty and after what seemed like hours of blind panic we were told to stand down, and pack it all away.

When the bodies were brought to the hospital the ambulances waited outside the A&E entrance; a doctor was designated to go out and certify their deaths. Seizing every opportunity as a chance to learn I asked to accompany him. Whether it was ghoulish intrigue, or whether I needed to be part of the process that had captivated me for those long hours. (for closure and completeness). I accompanied the young doctor, expecting to see a solemnly detailed process of certifying the death of the two men. I stepped into the ambulance to see the men responsible for the awful few hours I had experienced, the doctor flipped back the sheets of both men and exclaimed,

"Wow, definitely dead!"

Their injuries were obvious and they were without doubt dead. Important parts of them sat in a bucket. Only the hair visible informed you that what lay in the bucket constituted someone's head, and had belonged to one of the poor men. I had seen dead people before but all of whom I'd also known when alive. Death was often a blessing, an end to suffering and pain, but this was different, this was impersonal and cold. This was someone's son, father, brother, husband but we didn't know who. We merely acknowledged life had ended and sent them to the morgue.

Seeing the bodies, especially with their terrible injuries didn't upset me as much as the impersonal nature of A&E. With its constant stream of strangers, unknown diagnosis and the philosophy of patch them up and pass them on. This certainly wasn't a job for me.

Photos 1 to 7

Photo 1 – Kathleen Harris (July 1952). My Mum with her nursing group.

Photo 2 – Richard Salter SRN. My Dad on the left.

Photo 3 – Epsom District Hospital Nurses Home.
(Top photo – my room circled: Bottom photo –
Shortly before it was all demolished, a sad day)

Photo 4 – Feb '86 gang. From Left: Me, Amanda, Nina and Melanie

Photo 5 – Feb'86 intake: Fresh faced second years.

Photo 6 – Princess Margaret at Hackney Hospital
(My Parents are lost in the crowd)

Photo 7 – Celebrating the NHS's 50th Anniversary
(a bad hair day)

Death

Death is something you can get used to, the more you see, the more you realise death is usually much harder on those that are left behind. The majority of terminally ill people are eventually mentally ready to die. There is an acceptance and a need for release, especially if that time is filled with pain. It had often been my experience that the presence of loved ones at a bedside can prolong those last few hours. I have no idea of the scientific fact or research into this but, to my mind, hearing is the last sense to leave us therefore hearing our closest families' voices may be the last thing that tethers us. It is often the case that the moment the family leave or take a break the patient dies.

My mother nursed my dying father in their bed at home when I was four. He died of cancer aged forty-two and I would sit next to him, comatose, as we waited for the end. I still keep the get-well notes and pictures I drew him. My mother placed us on the bed when he could still speak, telling me to be a good girl and telling my six-year-old brother he was now going to be the man of the house and it was his job to look after his mother and his sister. Death held no mystery or horror for me, but being left, and living on without that person in your life is the greatest challenge. Of course, there is always fear around death because it is unknown. People have their beliefs of heaven, hell, reincarnation and Armageddon but none of us truly knows. It is the one equaliser and the one true certainty in life.

I am a huge fan of euthanasia or assisted dying, not the grey area where people choose to end their life prematurely or worse still being used by others to end someone else's life for their convenience. But for when all hope is gone. If you have ever watched someone die there is always the final phase, the time that there is no coming back from. And it is for these people I would love to see a kinder and a quicker release from suffering. I would never let any of my dogs suffer in the way I have seen countless human beings suffer.

I nursed my mother as she died, six months in my lounge in a hospital bed, and her final few days in the hospice we are so lucky to have nearby.

She was a Jehovah's Witness with leukaemia and as her oncologist rightly said on first meeting us,

"Really what the bloody hell am I supposed to do with you?"

She was given six weeks and she had six months. I left work and we laughed much more than we cried. She wrote letters to everyone special in her life, I have mine in my desk drawer as I write. She wrote her life story chronicling every name and detail she could recall. It was the most special time and I'm thankful to have had it with her.

But the day came, the day of no return and the marvellous GP visited, sitting on her commode he cried. He told us he thought it would be hours or at most a couple of days and her breathing was rattly and laboured and we could hear it from our beds. Six months had been all about my mum, the last days had to be about my teenage daughter in the midst of GCSEs and my ever-patient husband. I may be fine with death, but would they relax and laugh in the room Ganny had died in? Thankfully we were blessed and the hospice had a vacancy and was literally down the road so that afternoon, with much hilarity with the ambulance crew she was transferred. The attending doctor agreed with our GP that it was a matter of hours or days. So, no matter what you think you know about euthanasia I hope you never have to watch helplessly on as someone you love hovers between life and death. She was fit and hearty and that huge generous heart carried on beating for a further ten days. The ten nights I slept on a camp bed next to her, every morning she cried, cried because she had had enough. Cried because she couldn't move, or eat, but just lay there in an awful purgatory of waiting. All positive pleasure, all reason to live had faded.

My mum freely admitted when my father had reached this stage she gave him morphine, he was unresponsive and he lay in that limbo that there is never any coming back from. Apparently, she asked the GP at the time how much morphine could she give him, and his compassionate reply was, what ever you think he needs. If I could have done this for my mum in the end I would have, and if I have one regret about the care I gave her, it was the I couldn't hasten those last ten days.

I have lost four dogs, two cats and held them as they were put to sleep, it is the greatest final gift we can give to pets that we love. But for a beloved parent, fantastically courageous, brave, talented and kind human being we are just forced to sit back and watch.

In my years as a cancer nurse my goal was always to support and guide people to make this process as straightforward as possible. Grasp for every charity willing to help whether it's Macmillan or the local hospice. It is the only certain thing in our lives, we will all die. If we can we should do it with as little pain and as much humour and grace as we can muster.

Living With Nurses

But enough of this maudlin talk, let's head back to the nurses' home, to the 1980s, shoulder pads and bad perms.

The room I described earlier was just far too depressing to stay in. Whether it was the smell, the colour (I have always hated pink) or too much Clannad I pleaded with the housing officer to let me swap. The only empty room was on the other end of the third floor but isolated on its own surrounded by the stairwell, lift shaft and laundry room. It was larger than the other rooms and obviously, previously intended for someone grander than a student nurse (See Photo 9 & circled in Photo 3). Although its location rendered it fridge-like, it had the huge benefit of an upgraded electrical supply. It was a dirty blue colour, having a slightly less disgusting carpet, and my new home. All the other nurses suffered the frustration of queuing for the few plug sockets on the main corridor. Kettles, irons and hoovers all jockeyed for position at the half a dozen plug sockets.

Nurses would leave their appliances in a bizarre electrical queue, etiquette dictated when your kettle had boiled you plugged in the next. Although it never failed to amaze me, that a building full of students in the caring profession could be cold-hearted and mean and often this nicety wasn't adhered to. Occasionally you could hear the raised voices of a plug war in the corridor as one occupant would take exception to another's disregard for the queue system.

In the 80s a hospital was still run with almost military precision. Cleanliness was king and every bed space was washed thoroughly between patients. Not an ineffectual swipe with an alco wipe, this involved a large bowl of steaming hot soapy water. Every surface that a patient may have touched was scrubbed top, sides and underneath. We didn't have C Diff, wards were not closed for the NORO virus and we didn't have MRSA. (all modern-day hospital acquired super bugs). If the ward was quiet and you were caught standing, let alone sitting you were allocated something to clean. The sluice was a favourite but any wall, cupboard, surface or piece of equipment would be shining. It was unacceptable to sit down unless writing up your nursing notes. If you are confident, you had done all your work and all your patients needs were met you would wander around their beds tidying and chatting to prevent being caught and sent to the sluice.

As a qualified nurse of advancing years, I found it hard to shake this habit. If I saw junior members of staff sitting and chatting, I'm afraid they would be delegated a job. Once in endoscopy we had an unexpected closure of a theatre. I saw this as a splendid opportunity to wash the shelves and walls so asked the student nurse to help me. She replied she wasn't going to university to get a degree to wash walls. So rather than a short session in one room, myself and the student thoroughly cleaned the theatre and spent the next four hours washing trolley wheels.

It remains ingrained in me and when I'm a visitor or a patient in a ward I have a terrible urge to tidy and clean. Some may disagree, but by God standards have slipped. Bearing these lofty standards in mind I'm sure you will be surprised to hear what a disgusting mess the nurses' home was. Living in a building chock full of keen young nurses you would think the communal areas shone like new pins, nothing could be further from the truth! I suppose it is similar to being married to a decorator; apparently their houses rarely get painted. The inside of the nurses' home was an utter disgrace.

The building was originally a workhouse so no en suite facilities here. On the third floor which must have housed dozens of nurses there were three bathrooms. The one on the landing opposite my room was at least twenty feet square with a dark terracotta tiled floor almost black through lack of cleaning. There were no cleaners supplied by the hospital it was left up to the nurses in residence to do this, and not one chose to. Non-existent heating and high ceilings made for an echoey cold room. The paint on the ceiling was flaking, as you lay back lounging in a bath you could lose many minutes making patterns and faces out of the crumbling surface. In the centre of the room sat an enormous cast-iron bath, primrose yellow, and I had wondered when it was first built if it was designed to house more than one person, maybe when it was a workhouse you could squeeze four in.

The other bathrooms at the other end of the long corridor had been modernised sometime in the 70s. Baths were shoehorned alongside toilets in cubicles. I have often wondered who invented the cubicle with high bottoms and low tops, the sort that play out in nightmares when you are desperate to pee. I have always believed it is the subconscious mind preventing you from wetting the bed in your sleep. And these bathrooms were nightmarish and I never chose to frequent them.

Faded opulence was for me and I would lie and float in the bath and wait for my head or my toes to touch the ends. It was a luxury not often to be repeated and the hand-basin in our rooms became the preferred means of washing for most. For some reason I never truly understood, nurses steal things, anything that wasn't screwed down was game, including bath plugs.

Preparation for a bath involved at least a two-hour window to complete the mission. A good book, or if time was of the essence the essay you were working on was taken for the inevitable wait. Sitting on the floor in the corridor waiting for the selfish bitch who'd been soaking the ages. Armed with a good cleaning product, scouring sponge and toilet roll (because someone had stolen it) and all the usual bathroom accessories you were ready to try and get a bath. I kept mine in a bucket under my sink primed and ready to grab and run if I noticed the bathroom was empty. I think it had been many years since the hospital had given up cleaning the nurses' home and by mutual and silent agreement the nurses followed suit.

    I perfected a trick within the first few months after sticking to the unwashed floors, of folding my clothes so that they could be stored in my bucket during my ablutions. I am not a fussy person; I live in a house of clutter and well organised chaos but there is one thing I can't abide (probably a result of three years in that nurses' home) the feeling of bits under my feet. Sticky floors that grip your slippers I do find offensive and the solution kept me sane - paper towels. The hospital did supply thick murky green paper towels by the sinks of the communal areas. Judiciously placed across the floor they were the perfect stepping stones through the grime.

    Once in and the door safely bolted the task of cleaning the bath began and after a good rinse and the plug-in place you could start it running. It took ages to fill and you soon learnt to be deaf to the frequent bangs on the door and screaming at your selfishness. I have never appreciated bathing as much as when I finally got to have a soak in that fabulous bath, and for those few precious moments I became the bitch who soaked too long.

In my third year a block of showers was built on the second floor and we were really spoilt. All the girls in my group (or set) were local - Cheam, Sutton, Worcester Park and Epsom so frequently went home for the night or on their days off. Although just over an hour from home my nurse's wages wouldn't support weekly trips back to Portsmouth, but I am eternally grateful to the generosity of some of my dearest friend's parents. Often, I would go home with a friend if on similar shifts and enjoy a home-cooked meal and a much-appreciated use of a bathroom that didn't require a scouring pad, Jiff and stepping on paper towels.

Wages? Yes, you read it right we had a salary! Back then you were paid by the hospital to be a student nurse. It wasn't as altruistic a gesture as you might think, for the princely sum of £200 a month you worked 37 ½ hour week, doing any shift pattern that suited the ward you were assigned to. There was none of this, 'I don't like to work Fridays' or 'I'd like every weekend off', you worked when you were needed - end of. It was an absolute treat to be given two consecutive days off together. £40 was deducted a month for the salubrious accommodation and with the rest we managed to run a car and eat.

This brings me neatly to idiotic idea number seven. Living on site, literally within spitting distance to work was the perfect situation. Yet again fall out from disastrous idea number 1. Not only were you close at hand with no travel expenses, there was no need to pay for parking. I have worked night shifts since qualifying and frankly am surprised, to still be alive to tell the tale. How extremely dangerous it is to drive after being at work for eleven hours at night. We didn't appreciate it then, but I for one, was undressing and emptying my uniform as I clanked up in the lift to my desperately anticipated bed. Ward to bed in less than five minutes, you can't put a price on that.

Now Universities may have practical placements at numerous hospitals in their catchment area. The students may have to work at multiple hospitals during their training. Student nurses are not exempt and will face hefty car parking charges for every shift they do. Finishing a late shift to drive home to your expensive accommodation only to have to be up horribly early for the next days early shift. Forget about public transport, shift work and buses and trains are not compatible.

You had enormous support from your peers and you had no pressure or fear for your finances. Who on earth thought doing away with nurses' homes and living in universities overpriced accommodation (plus the cost of £9000 a year), was in any way a good idea. Student nurses I have stated already in my experience have sub-standard practical knowledge, huge financial pressures but most importantly have lost the camaraderie and support that sustained us.

Now student nurses live in accommodation with a mixture of other students, whether studying the arts and languages, or any other subject taught at that University. Sadly, none of whom can have a shared experience of their hospital placements. No matter how awful a shift, how difficult an essay, or the first time you see someone die, for us, there was a huge support network right there in your home.

Nursing as you may well appreciate is bloody hard sometimes and being able to run back to the safety of your room surrounded by peers who are navigating their way through the strange and often frightening world of nursing helped immensely in getting you through it. I am so sorry for young nurses now who have had that huge support network taken away from them.

I now regret not taking a photograph of the nurses' home kitchen, I would love to add it to this book. So let me paint you a picture, hopefully it will be as if you were there. For three years I lived in my little blue room. It was always cold, even in summer, but it was a safe place and often full of laughter and the place to gather. Due to my upgraded electricity supply not only could I boil a kettle whenever the hell I liked, my array of electric gadgets grew. I pushed my luck and in the end was the envy of all with an electric heater, a one ring element, a toaster and even a mini cooker (credits to my wonderful cousins Jean and Bob who bought this for me).

I could rustle up scrambled eggs on toast as if by magic and as my gadgets increased my need to use the one kitchen on my corridor diminished, it was a huge blessing.

Three summers passed and no one had cleaned it. The sash windows were permanently jammed full open to try and deal with the smell. The two gas cookers, that even if you covered your food with foil didn't feel enough protection from the puddles of who knows what and the grease encrusted grime. It didn't help as the main user of the kitchen was an African nurse, she was shy but always smiled and I'd never worked with her so had no opinion on her nursing skills but had great reservations about her culinary ones. One day a stench that had heads peering from their rooms the length of the corridor compelled me to investigate. Marching up to the kitchen the smell grew stronger as I approached. Even the open window hadn't helped and the prevailing wind was wafting the stench down the corridor and swirling it under our doors. I gingerly opened the oven door; it took a few seconds for my brain to assimilate the vision before me. On a large baking tray was a tongue, you could clearly see the taste buds, cow I presumed. Alongside it, two feet or hooves, each to their own and I'm sure she was going to whip up culinary delights but that was the last time I ever touched the cooker.

  For at least the second half of my time in the nurses' home I didn't use the kitchen at all but I would always stop to look in as I passed on the way to my friends' rooms. At some point someone on the television had said you can tell if spaghetti is cooked if it sticks to the wall. I wonder if they knew the beast they unleashed but it became a sort of art installation. The greasy flaking paint on the walls now supported strands of rigid petrified spaghetti. Like stalactites they hung across the ceiling and clung to the walls.

Real testament to the hospital's neglect and the slovenly residents was during the third long hot summer of the blocked sink. Like the rest of the building the original structures were well built but had never been modernised. The sink was a beast, originally white but grazed and chipped now a murky grey. It stood under the window on sturdy legs - a huge ancient butler sink. If it hadn't been so filthy you could have skipped the two-hour bathroom queue and bathed in it.

It became a talking point, a science experiment that last summer I lived at Epsom. It had blocked, with what no one knew, or was brave enough to investigate. Full to the brim with brown water, peas and spaghetti floating in the layer of grease. This is how it stayed for many weeks, fly Nirvana. "Dirty bitches" was the frequent murmur of nurses walking past. I was never more grateful for my upgraded electric, and my need to never enter the kitchen again.

Midwifery

The room I called home looked out over one of the hospital car parks, which was small and surrounded by trees and not an unpleasant outlook. The building opposite my window was the maternity wing. This I could have lived without. Mine was the only room on the third floor facing this way and I had the unenviable position of being able to look straight into the labour rooms opposite. On a hot day, with only a road width between our windows; I could sit on my bed trying to watch the new Australian soap opera Neighbours accompanied by the screams of women giving birth.

Recalling my experiences of midwifery I open with an apology, an unreserved sorry to all the good and compassionate midwives out there. In all my experiences as a student nurse and a patient, the majority are heartless bitches. Too harsh I hear you cry! But I can only judge as I find, and the midwives I worked with as a student nurse did nothing to make me feel differently or change my opinion.

I wonder in a speciality of bringing joy and life into the world, why there should be such an element of heartlessness. Maybe you have to be tough to spend day in, and day out, listening to women screaming in pain and think that that's okay. I have never been a fan of childbirth; it seems terrifying and barbaric. I am certain if men gave birth by the time of Victoria, pushing out a baby, ripping your pelvic floor to shreds and screaming in pain would be a thing of the past. We don't amputate legs with a shot of whiskey and a leather strap to bite on any more, the whole thing baffles me.

Having spent balmy summers evenings with my window closed and my TV volume turned up to drown out the screams, it was with much trepidation I started my 10-week stint in maternity. I was in my second year and confident enough in the basics but well aware I knew nothing about childbirth. I think my biggest issue is the midwife's mantra, "You are not sick, you're having a baby".

Speaking as one who had pre-eclampsia and nearly died this statement offends me. If you are not medically trained, the fact that you have drunk nine litres of water and have passed thirteen mls into your catheter bag is not because it is 'warm in here' which was one reaction from a midwife from my genuine fears that my kidneys were no longer working. A temperature of 38.2° C is not 'because you have your cardigan on', it is a dangerous infection. But enough about my near-death experiences and appalling care at the hands of midwives when I was a patient, back to Epsom.

As previously mentioned, a nurse's hand over is often a brutal vent between staff.

"Well, I'm not looking after her, she is seven days postpartum she needs to get up and look after her baby and go home." A qualified midwife's reaction to caring for one particular lady.

So true to form, I offered to look after the lady in the cubicle who no one else seemed to like. I liked the idea of doing what I knew and hopefully, with a seven-day-old baby the mother should know what to do with it, as I certainly had no idea. The smell hit you as you entered the room, half the population will know what I mean, the gents will have to give it their best guess, sweaty sanitary towels. For seven days this traumatised young woman had laid flat on her back. Her baby, healthy and squirming in a cot next to her seemed content so my full attention was on the mother.

She explained that it was her first baby and her and her husband had waited years for this day. They had been so excited but for the past seven days it had been a hideous nightmare. She had opted for an epidural, where a fine needle is passed between the spinal bones and an anaesthetic is injected, numbing you from the injection site down. I have never had one myself, but have witnessed a few, and for my money would rather be knocked out. For this unlucky lady it had gone wrong. The fluid in your spinal column lubricates it and there was a small reservoir in your brain. A person can afford to lose a few precious drops of this fluid and the body will replenish it over time. But if you deprive it of too much fluid, the human body has a marvellous fail-safe, it will not let you lift your head. Any attempt to lift your head even an inch above your body results in excruciating pain and nausea.

Somehow, someone had deprived this lady's brain of its crucial fluid and seven days after giving birth she was literally pinned to the sheets. Turning her head slowly and even an inch to try and see her baby resulted in scream inducing pain. She hadn't planned for this, no prenatal classes could prepare you for this. The hospital and its staff had caused this and what was their response? "Lazy bitch, she just needs to get on with it."

Shocking isn't it, I'm still shocked to this day, I wonder was she ever brave enough to risk going through pregnancy again? We didn't discuss PTSD then, not for a medical experience, but if ever someone was entitled to a dose of PTSD it was that poor lady. My own experiences at the hands of midwifery deterred me from ever having more children, and I had nowhere near such an awful experience as this young woman.

I set about doing all I could to make her comfortable, give her some relief from this torture. When all else fails bring out the big bed bath. I started at her sweaty hair and worked my way down. Blood still streaked her legs and crusted in the small of her back. I will save you the gory details but over a bedpan it took many bowls of water to deal with the carnage post birth. She cried and apologised for the smell and the state she was in. She cried for not being able to tend to her baby, with the added insult of staff making her feel quite guilty every time she buzzed her call bell when her baby cried.

At the end of the shift, I burst into the first available friend's room and that night I cried, I drank cheap wine and my mistrust and hatred of midwives was born, it is mine, I own it, if it offends you, tough.

I managed to witness three births from start to finish, all totally different. The Vietnamese lady who spoke no English was a very orderly affair. Her husband sat silently in the corner of the room with two small children beside him. The only way I knew birth was imminent was the regularity and spiking on the monitor tracking her contractions. She neither spoke, nor grimaced, and without words and one 'tooth-gritting' push, she shot out baby number three.

The second birth, I stayed on over when my shift was due to finish to see it to completion. As I came on duty in the morning the bubbly blonde girl, (as she was my age) and her dustbin man husband arrived. She had scented candles and a tape recorder with her favourite music. She had her birth plan and was convinced she was in charge. Ten hours later I think I was as exhausted as they were. Scented candles in the bin, cassette recorder thrown on the floor and the couple had moved seamlessly from the excited, loved up phase into the psychotic phase.

From affirming gentle words of love to her screaming,

"I hate you, this is your bloody fault!"

Finally, it ended with them cuddling their new baby girl, and an overwhelming sense of joy and relief for everyone in the room. The shift had started by her regaling me with tales of their courtship and wedding and how in love they were. I think it was four hours in when she was thumping his tattooed shoulder and digging her long nails maliciously into his fist with a vice-like grip.

Maternity services seemed to me a conveyor belt of pain and angst, with huge emotions of elation, love and amnesia at the end.

The last case that resonated with me started in the outpatient department. I sat in the back of the room and listened to the obstetrician as he examined bumps, and listened to foetal heartbeats with his little trumpet. It was quite dull; pregnancy didn't interest me having never thought I would want to put myself through it. I went to the waiting room to call in the next patient. Most sat banally smug, smiling and flicking through magazines but there was something different, uptight about this lady. She was nervous that was obvious, and clearly, no expert I could see she was heavily pregnant. Sitting opposite the doctor's desk she rubbed her belly constantly.

"Could we just get it out now, I really want it out now?"

And so, the story unfolded, she had suffered a few miscarriages and the previous year had gone full term and delivered a dead baby. A fully formed 'stillbirth' that no-one could explain why, or, give her any closure on. She clearly was desperate to get this one out while it was still alive. I didn't know her; I obviously knew nothing about midwifery but had to restrain myself from shouting out and joining her protestations.

"Just get it out now!"

The doctor reassured her as best he could and a caesarean was booked for the following week. I could only imagine her counting down the days, the fear was so obvious in her face, it was palpable. The ward I worked on agreed I could go and be present for this. The day arrived and I tucked myself in the back of the theatre to watch the scene unfold. There was a full house, the patient obviously and her husband clung to each other behind a paper screen and around them a very well-oiled team. There is a look, a glance. They don't teach it in class but it is universal in medicine,

"Get ready, this could go horribly wrong."

Inside your head is screaming, "Shit, shit, this is going horribly wrong! Don't let them die!" But your demeanour is calm, your voice reassuring and you give your colleagues 'the look'. It is acknowledged, you have to step up and do your bit. Glances were darting from surgeons to the paediatric resuscitation team loitering around an incubator, and the more than usual number of midwives in the room.

The shaking student in the corner is ignored and that suited me just fine. I had been given a job before the patient entered and I clutched the clipboard and pen like a shield and a dagger. One job, who knew Caesareans were so quick, obviously not me. From the moment the scalpel cut through her skin and a big screaming baby was hoisted out seemed like seconds. I looked down on the page, the time of the first incision, time of birth, time cord cut et cetera et cetera were all blank except for splats from my tears. There wasn't a dry eye in the room and the heavy dread of anticipation morphed into elation and joy as the paediatric team rubbed, suctioned and presented a healthy baby girl to its sobbing parents.

I write longhand in a book, with the pen, yes, I'm that old, so when you read this, it will have been typed up and you won't see the teardrops on the page as I remember that day. It is as real and as powerful all these years later and hopefully somewhere is a woman in her late thirties completely unaware her birth is being remembered in this book.

So, three cheers to the maternity service! Bringing our most precious possessions into the world, for the most part when everything is going to plan the service works, and women go back to have more than one child (mad fools, but not me). For my own experience I found the most callous nurses I have worked with were to be found in midwifery. It was always the case that to be a midwife you first qualify as a general nurse. Now that can be skipped, and there is direct entry to train to be a midwife. I don't presume to know anywhere near enough of the calibre or thoroughness of their training, but things change not always for the best. Certainly, from my own experience when I was very unwell, I wanted my midwife to be a nurse as well.

Achilles Heel

Every nurse has one, the one thing that is distasteful, objectionable and downright disgusting to them. For me it is eyes. During our training students worked in nearly every ward in the hospital. The two areas I avoided were eyes and intensive care. I never much cared for gadgetry and a bank of machines that went 'bing' didn't interest me, so I was not sorry to miss that experience. But managing to get away without working with eyes I was eternally grateful for.

The one case I remember, that always makes me cringe involved a small ex-jockey. I would always beg to be relieved of caring for him; I could handle the abusive language and the poorly aimed thumps. He had dementia and it wasn't his fault, and I could duck. But every shift I would plead with my colleagues and even offer to work their night shifts if only someone else would remove his glass eye and clean it. Obviously, no one would, and poking your finger into an eye socket to flick it out and then trying to wriggle it back in was enough to have me gagging.

There are nurses who find vomit, blood, sputum or faeces most bothersome, my least favourite would be sputum and knew a career in respiratory wasn't for me. I was born to be a nurse, whether being the third generation in the profession resulting from some Darwinian evolution; or just good luck I am blessed with a terrible sense of smell. Unless I make a concerted effort and breathe deeply through my nose, I can pretty much avoid most smells.

The biggest test of this came on our visit to the morgue. Everyone in medicine should see a post-mortem, doctors in their training get to play with pickled parts of bodies but for a nurse to actually see inside a body makes all the textbooks and diagrams make sense.

We were encouraged to go, so fresh faced and mildly afraid we walked in groups of six to eight over to meet the mortician. There were two men, one of which had Marty Feldman eyes and a mad scientist hair do. We knew him already as he often burst open the door into the main corridor as we entered the building, with the desired effect of making us jump. On entering the morgue my first impression was a surprise, the staff were chatty and friendly. The gallows humour and banter that is shared in the hospital is very well utilised in a morgue. Music played and it was as if the staff were blissfully unaware dead bodies were lying on stainless steel beds around them.

Most of us had seen a dead body by the time we visited but the huddle of pale blue uniforms reluctantly moved towards the old man on the slab. The mortician, or is it pathologist I'm not sure which, stood on the other side of the old man and started to talk us through the procedure. Pulling the Scalp forward like thin pastry to reveal the skull, the mortician had thankfully done before we arrived. With a circular saw he then proceeded to cut the top of the skull off like a hard-boiled egg. That did for one of the group who rushed out to vomit. There was a fainter who was caught before she could do any damage and taken to the office and much mouth holding and utterings of disgust.

I found myself edging forward, and the mortician excited to have someone show an interest beckoned me to him.

"Look we cut the tongue and lift out the upper GI tract" he said eagerly, as I leaned in as the oesophagus and stomach could be visualised. There was some retching from the girls behind me and one of my friends called.

"Anne how can you bear the smell?"

"What smell?"

And then it happened, with my head halfway inside the open cavity of the corpse I took a deep breath. It was a struggle from then on and the mortician had lost his keenest pupil as I slowly edged back the safety of the remaining group.

For every ward there will be things you hate and staff you dislike but equally patients that touched your heart, and staff that invested in you to make you a better nurse. It was the greatest of apprenticeships and working on so many areas gave you an insight and knowledge for so many things.

Nowadays (here she goes again I hear the young cry) it seems nurses have little glimpses, and tasters of what it is to be a nurse and then, there they are, with a degree. A fully qualified nurse in charge of patient care. From all I hear from young nurses it is a terrifying position to be in. We were afraid, don't get me wrong but we had trained three hard, hands-on years. What scared us were the new responsibilities of drug rounds and ward management the rest we had been well tested on and had in the bag. All too often I hear newly qualified nurses wanting to specialise, rise through the ranks, get out into the community because the ward in a busy hospital is too terrifying a place to be. Of course it is, because they have been let down and not properly prepared. Take your time, you have so much to learn yet, and hopefully have a long successful career ahead of you. My advice to newly qualified nurses has always been to work on the hardest, busiest ward you can find and hone your skills. Be a good basic nurse before you search for glamour of the specialism and a higher pay band, it's no less scary up there.

Working in any profession for thirty-seven years you will see change. Usually instigated by a manager with pounds and not patients as their priority, often with no benefit for the patient let alone the staff.

Let's take observation charts, as old as nursing, there has always been a paper document attached to a patient's bed charting the essentials. Pulse, blood pressure, temperature and respiratory rate; clear, concise a universal record. It is highly visible, attached to the end of the bed, and an essential tool for medical personnel. As a good nurse you should be able to look at a patient from the foot of their bed, check their chart and assess the whole. The temperature may have been steadily rising, their pulse today, on average, is faster, they look flushed and are vague when questioned and already alarm bells are ringing. On the sheet of paper you can see bowel habits, they haven't had their bowels open for days, you look at their catheter, the urine is cloudy. Have they drunk enough? You consult the fluid chart.

You didn't need a laminated algorithm or a palm pad computer to tell you they have an infection, probably a urinary infection exacerbated by their dehydration and constipation. You certainly don't need to wait for a computer program to tell you to dip test urine, send off a sample, encourage lots of fluids(drinks) and investigate further and inform the team of nurses and doctors directly looking after he patient.

But now, whether derived from failings of staff or a backhander from the managers, someone is sitting very rich on a beach after the hospital has switched over to this computerised package. Will there be enough palm pads, are they charged and available? Of course not, this is the NHS. Welcome to idiotic idea eight making the NHS paperless.

A nurses first line of assessment is now not right in front of her face (more importantly not beside the patient). It is stored on an electronic device and if you don't work on the ward or have forgotten your password that door is closed to you. As a specialist nurse for many years, this was a blatantly obvious change, for no benefit. Visiting a patient on the ward whom I may never have previously met before; these charts gave me a tangible insight into that patient's wellbeing, an overview and baseline to plan care. But, without consultation or warning one of my skills was removed. Like a finger had been cut off. The truly sad thing is, they (whoever thought it was a good idea) don't know, or care that they have done it. It is wholly detrimental to patient care and an obscene waste of money. Plough the funds back into resourceful, well-educated carers instead.

Moving swiftly on to another ridiculous result of idiotic idea eight. This year my hospital introduced computerised drug trolleys WTF! The traditional drug trolley hadn't changed design for decades, for good reason, it worked. The new drug trolley is an ergonomic disaster. The computer keyboard and screen are at a good height on a movable trolley, but now the nurses have to bend and twist, peering into a dark box to try and find drugs underneath. Designed and introduced by bean counters yet again. Were nurses consulted? Of course not.

I witnessed an extremely proficient ward sister trying to use the system who was near to tears. She said it was awful but they had been told they had to trial it. Being the NHS, hers and many more negative feedback will be swept under the carpet and contracts signed. Condemning even more nurses to just a little more stress and more sickness due to bad backs.

I am sure it is a boon for the pharmacy department, for their audit and restocking, which I'm sure is the only advantage to its introduction. For the nurse who has to navigate a complicated and confusing program it brings no benefit. It was probably hailed and sold as a safer means of giving medicine, which, in every way it isn't. The same nurse has to read, pick up, dish out, the correct drug to the correct patient, none of this has changed.

Many have tried to make the NHS paperless. Big IT companies promised it in the 90s, and certain applications and programmes are a boon. When I had a new cancer patient, a few minutes scrolling through letters and results on the computer could be completed whilst chatting to the patient on the phone. But crucially until the NHS has the resources to have a computer screen on the end of every bed (You could employ thousands of nurses for the cost of that – just saying!) leave the paper charts alone. They serve a greater function than any manager will ever comprehend.

"My Parkinson's patient doesn't look right."

It isn't scientific, it is a gut instinct backed up by years of experience. This patient can't or won't answer me and it is crucial he has his medicine at precisely the right time. Hang on I'll check his paper chart at the end of his bed. These charts have been designed and perfected to tell you all you need to know. A small cross and code letter in his lunchtime dose, and the excuse, "not given, off the ward" tells you all you needed to know. Within a matter of seconds you have solved the problem, know what you have to do to remedy it, and can act. But now the robotic drug trolley has replaced the chart and has to be found, so you waste valuable minutes wandering the ward to find another nurse is halfway through navigating the non, user-friendly system. Interrupting her is not acceptable mid case, so you stand and twiddle your fingers hoping the system isn't too slow today. Before you would have grabbed the keys, found the drugs and taken them straight to the patient.

They have done it again, removed another tool from our toolbox costing the NHS millions. I am not a dinosaur who is afraid of change, but vehemently opposed to change, for change's sake. All too often these changes are made for financial gain, or by a manager with no practical medical experience wanting to make a name for themselves by some new initiative. As a nurse you soon learn and reach the sad realisation you are but a tiny cog, in an enormous machine, designed and run by people who have not the first concept or understanding of what you do.

Hacking of hospital computers is for the scum of the earth a new hobby. When a bunch of keys and a pile of paper drug charts were at your disposal, systems could glitch and go off line but no patient need be delayed their pain medicine. The doctor writes it, the nurse administers it, and the patient takes it; nothing could or should ever interfere with this. Well not any more, welcome to technology that has improved absolutely nothing. Well done, hope you are proud of yourselves.

Resuscitation

Something that has altered little in many years is resuscitation. Every year, so thirty-seven of them, I have attended resuscitation training. It is part of all mandatory training everyone who works in a hospital must attend. A few hours in a classroom with poor old 'Resusci Annie' and my ever-declining knees. At my last training I admitted defeat and asked for my dummy to be placed on a table. It was not my proudest moment, and helped make the decision it was time to hang up my stethoscope. I am well aware that, if the need arose, I would throw myself to the floor to try and save a life, I'd give it a go. These days I don't kneel for any reason now including practising resuscitation.

I only recently learnt that the face of Annie was taken from an actual death mask of a girl who had died in the river Seine in 1900. What a thought, that your legacy was the image of your face being kissed by millions of people all over the world.

During my short stint as a practice educator, I had the dubious honour of working in the simulation suite. It is a training suite for doctors and nurses and has full size dummies; one of which looks like my brother's childhood action man only six foot tall. Connected to a computer operated by a James Bond villain – oh sorry an anaesthetist, behind a two-way mirror. Students would then be put through their paces. The patient, he was no Annie, he looked more like an Arnie, could breathe; well, his chest would rise and fall and he could open and close his eyes. His observations monitor was controlled from the Booth.

Now call me old-fashioned (I'm sure you have already) but get a member of staff to play the part. I'm sure with some amateur dramatic aspirations it would be cheaper, more realistic and much less creepy. There were cringe-making hours I will never get back, watching a group of young doctors take it in turns to assess Arnie. The anaesthetist controlled the mannequin teasing them along the path of diagnosing sepsis (life threatening infection) or deep vein thrombosis (blood clot in leg). Watching the screen with their colleagues in another room as they all shouted advice that couldn't be heard.

The act of resuscitation been a constant. Every few years they will change the rates and the ratio of breaths to compressions; backed, I'm sure on scientific research or just to confuse. For all the research and all the science, Vinnie Jones singing 'Staying Alive' will be, I'm sure, what I will think about if I'm ever in that situation again. When I first started nursing you led with a thump. Obviously, you would start with some gentle shoulders shaking, and for the drinkers and fakers, a firm pinch of the ear lobe, that's soon sorts them out.

"Are you all right, can you hear me?" Thump. One assertive bang on the centre of the chest just in case your patient was actually asleep, and if not, it may revive them. But those days are gone and this step has been eliminated. Now we are worried about our safety the safety of others and it's all about assessing the hazards. Now I'm not saying this is a bad thing but I'm afraid in an emergency I do believe I would thump someone before I thought about the consequences.

You are actively discouraged now from giving mouth-to-mouth. In the hospital you will find small masks with filters you can place over someone's face and breath for them in the event of them not being able to do it themselves. But the guidance is, if not in hospital, not to do it. Whether this is based on research that it is ineffective, or because too many people have sued, or been sued for catching some disease. I'm not sure but I think probably the latter, and probably due largely to HIV and AIDS that terrified us back in the day and our new friend Covid 19 of course.

I probably will never do this training again, but knees willing, I'd have a go at chest compressions and probably mouth-to-mouth as it is surely better than nothing. It was a badge of honour during my training to be involved in a cardiac arrest. Like putting in a catheter or pulling out a drain, the more you did, the better you got at it and the less frightening it was for all. I had in three years, a skill unrivalled by any of my counterparts, the skill of not being on duty when a patient had a cardiac arrest. I lost count of the times I would arrive for a late shift to the chaos of a passing storm.

"You've just missed it, man in bed ten arrested" or "As soon as you left yesterday the lovely lady in bed four died, we tried for ages but couldn't get her back."

To say I was pleased is an understatement, I was delighted! High octane was not my style and I never wanted to be in that club. A cardiac arrest call is put out for any person who has collapsed and has stopped breathing. Whether this was caused by a heart attack, a blood clot, choking or a host of reasons they are treated the same. Every bed space has an emergency buzzer which strikes ice in the veins of any nurse. Immediate staff do what they can, prepare the area, curtain off the patient, lay them flat then start what you've been trained to do ABC. Airway, breathing, cardiac compressions. The algorithm has changed of course, letters of been added and taken away but the basic premise is the same.

    The most important thing that any ward worker will agree is to get the 'crash team' there as soon as humanly possible. They have always existed, a team of specialist nurses, doctors and anaesthetists who take it in turns to carry the 'crash bleep'. Someone from the ward phones the switchboard who will bleep the team and wherever they are in the hospital, they come running. Hospital policy is, and always has been, no running. The only exception to this is the poor sod with the bleep. If ever you see someone running you open the doors to clear their path and hope, this time let them be successful, let them get the patient back.

I was getting nervous; I was on my last ward as a third year. Within weeks I would be qualified and I had never been present for a cardiac arrest. It serves me right as I had actually said it out loud.

"I hope I see one while I'm still a student."

It was bad enough to experience it first time as a senior student, but my mortal fear was to be qualified and for people to expect me to know what I was doing.

I was on a male respiratory ward, not my favourite place to be with the overflowing sputum pots, but I had weathered it reasonably well up to now. Being so absorbed in revising for final exams being on the ward felt like a bit of a rest. It was lunchtime and we were short staffed, having a charge nurse (a male ward sister), a first-year student nurse and myself. The charge nurse was busy with a drug round and I was helping the first-year do observations. She hadn't mastered blood pressures so I was checking up on her. There was an almighty crash and shouting at the entrance to the ward from the three bedded room. Two beds faced an exterior wall and windows but the bed nearest the entrance faced out onto the corridor.

The patient, whose name I can't remember, which I obviously wouldn't share with you, but unusual for me not to recall. I think because I've blocked it out of my memory. He was large, loud, and funny, and I do remember he was a market trader and he had the thickest gold necklace I've ever seen on a man. He had stood, (so his roommate shared with us) and had pulled the curtain so that he could use his bottle to pee. He must have needed to go because now it lay on the floor beside him. A twenty plus stone man had fallen face down across the threshold of the room, half in and half out onto the main corridor. He was surrounded by an enormous puddle of urine and the curtain he had ripped from its rail in the ceiling.

My brute force and the strong-armed charge nurse, between us managed to turn him on his back. There was nothing for it but to kneel in the pee, and my uniform of blue-and-white checked, thick polyester cotton, acted as a litmus paper. As we worked to revive him the urine, cold and clammy crept up my dress and stockings.

It felt surreal, and the charge nurse shouted orders as it was going to be visiting time soon. The first year was tasked with getting portable screens to put at the main door to the ward to cover the windows as we had no other means of shielding the patient from their view. A hastily written note, "do not enter ward closed" was fixed to the screen.

I knew the theory and the charge nurse knew his stuff. The student looked like a frightened rabbit and there was a longer delay getting the call out to the crash team so we worked on. My role was to do chest compressions, he was a big man. Resusci Annie clicks reassuringly when you get it right, he was big, hairy and squishy. Something that no one had warned me about was when you press, especially if someone else has just filled the patient's lungs, he moans, the air leaving his body made a rattling gasp. It was to say the least, really bloody off putting.

"Don't stop, just keep going!" The charge nurse screamed at me.

It seemed like hours but suddenly the thunder of feet up the stairwell and through the ward as the cavalry arrived. The crash team stood around and at the time I thought they must be so impressed with my technique as no one offered to take over. With hindsight it was obviously futile and no one wanted to kneel in the piss.

The day descended from thereon. We finally gave up and he had died. I wanted to run back to my room, strip off and shower and drink alcohol but instead there was a ward of sick respiratory patients that had been ignored and a queue of irate relatives demanding access and an explanation.

We had no hover jacks or hoists then, so four porters and as many of the crash team as we could squeeze around the body hauled him onto the bed. The poor two patients trapped in his room could have no visitors and sat sadly behind their curtains lamenting their jovial cellmate. Then came the job of last offices or laying out and I willingly volunteered. At least it would be just me, him and the chaps behind the curtain having a peaceful few moments away from the commotion on the ward. The adrenaline slowly dissipated as I washed him. Shoes were wet, my stockings and uniform sodden to the waist, what with this and the residual shock of the event I was shaking like a leaf. The charge nurse instructed me to go to my room, change, get some fresh air but be back in 15 minutes. I wanted to cry but was just too shaken so I walked slowly over to the nurses' home. It was winter I remember and the cold and damp clothes were a horrid reminder as they stuck to my legs.

I crossed the road and looked up; my expression easy to read.

"You seen a ghost love?"

The man walking towards me was the image of the dead man I had just left.

"No… I think you need to come with me."

I turned around and walked back with him to the ward. It was his brother, and I, still stood in my wet clothes. So, there it was, my first cardiac arrest, we learned later he had died from a massive blood clot and nothing we could have done would have helped. It helped us though, that need to know why you failed, it helps. It makes me sigh writing this because it was a hard day and etched deep in my memories and although unbelievable, it was only going to get worse.

I had seen grieving people, in my own life and when patients died but what I had never witnessed until that day was uncontrolled rage brought on by grief. The patient's brother had visited and I stood by him and rubbed his shoulder as he wept. I was glad I had laid the patient out, to me, now he looked peaceful in bed. A drastic difference to a few hours earlier spread-eagled surrounded by urine. The brother composed himself and called the man's children, two daughters and a son were on their way. Usually, you would leave the body for the family to view, but today was 'one of those unlucky days'.

The charge nurse's concern now was focused wholly on the remaining patients. The first priority being the two trapped men, either would have to walk past the deceased to get to the toilet. It was during the act of trying to transfer the body into the metal box, that transports the deceased to the morgue, his three children came bursting onto the ward. Demanding to see their father and shouting for answers, I was ordered to keep them in the bathroom opposite their father's room as the tricky task of moving him was not complete.

They paced, and they shouted.

"You killed him, what did you do?"

I stood all seven and a half stone, a shaking, urine-soaked wreck as the siblings, like caged animals milled around the small bathroom. They looked like their father especially the son, large and dark, and a good amount of gold flashed on them all.

"Let us see him, you can't stop us!"

It happened in a second and I was mute to react as the youngest daughter. taller than me by a good five inches and twice the weight had her hands around my neck. I wanted to scream but petty excuses whispered out from me.

"I tried, I tried. It was awful look I was kneeling in his pee to try and save your dad I'm sorry, I tried." Such was my state of shock I merely stood there until her siblings jumped in and hauled her off. They then turned on each other and I edged out of the room.

I spent the whole evening crying, being consoled and I'm sure consumed too much cheap wine. That was our well-being sorted and back to work I went the next day to carry on.

That was probably without doubt the worst day in my nursing career. I have been fortunate in all these years to witness very few arrests but sadly every single one ended in death. Is there a correlation you think? I think not, as I'm always more than willing to let someone more experienced step in.

I do have to shout out to a friend, a brave and courageous lady who has successfully resuscitated her husband in their home with no crash trolley or crash team to help. Not once but twice! Her actions humble me, her husband forgives the broken ribs and he is still here today because of her actions. All hail my friend Sally.

Cancer

For the last decade of my career, it has all been about cancer. It started as mentioned before, with my mother, nursing her in the front room by far the best work I've done. And when it was over I collapsed. It had long been planned, a holiday with my beautiful nurse friends from Epsom, for a week in Spain to celebrate our 25th anniversary. After the last babies were born and were old enough to be left with their fathers we started a tradition. Every February fifth, or nearest weekend to it we went away. Around the country we had enjoyed many fabulous weekends, now old hands our requirements were set: large sofas, log burner, and a hot tub are all nonnegotiable.

With at least four bedrooms, with a joke that never gets old, the rooms are allocated. Melanie is in charge, a quick dark humour inherited from her London cab driver father never fails to have us crying with laughter. What started with pulling straws has grown into elaborate word searches, quizzes and pass the parcel. Notes explaining the room you have been allocated include such gems as;

"Jammy bitch! Double en suite"

"Ha ha, pauper, you get the bunks!"

The tradition continues and 2026 will see our 40th anniversary so hoping we are all semi-continent, mobile and not too gaga to enjoy it. The expression 'You will always have to be my friend, because you know too much' was never truer.

So back to our 25th anniversary, our February meet was postponed due to my mother's illness. She had been given six weeks to live and the fact that she made six months was fantastic. I was a research nurse at the time, and the hospital and my bosses were very supportive. I could easily have taken sick leave or unpaid leave. I have always struggled with being off sick, I think it was so ingrained in our training, even with a raging temperature sweating under my duvet I feel guilty if I phone in sick. I personally could never take time off sick for stress, as it would be far too stressful being at home, worrying about not being at work. I opted instead to just walk away, handing in my notice, I quit. With hindsight it was the best thing I could have done, as it allowed me to be free, to concentrate 100% on my mother and my family, and after she had died, myself.

The six months with her in the lounge were precious and full of humour. My husband threatened to charge her rent if she lived over the six weeks and she gleefully would shout out as he went off to bed, 'no rent yet' when she had outlived her allotted time. Caring for her taught me two things, firstly, deadlines (pardon the pun) can be useful, or dangerous, and secondly use that time well. Six weeks I thought, I can do this! That fateful day when the oncologists told myself, my brother and my mother we hatched a plan. Within two days favours were called in and friends rallied, and she was wheeled over the threshold. My furniture was taken to her flat and her recliner chair appeared and she was extremely comfortable. A hospital bed, wheelchair, commode and a hoist completed the picture and so our days rolled into each other.

Leukaemia was kind to Kathleen, it was a painless and gentle decline. Her strength ebbed away until she was the ghost of her previous vivacious and strong self. Our routine was set, I would get up and shower and make us breakfast. We would chat and eat letting the morning light in. We discovered Judge Judy, the perfect companion as I would bed bath her, often having to refill the small yellow bowl with hot water as we would get so distracted with the juicy case. Once hoisted into her chair she would insist on trying to brush her hair whilst I tidied. The simple act of brushing her sparse hair was a monumental effort for her.

    The day came, as I discussed earlier when talking about euthanasia; there is a time and a phase you don't come back from. There would be no more playing cards no matter how slowly, no more enjoying a television programme together or enjoying her music. She knew the time had come and there were to be no more visitors, and with a huge relief we headed for the hospice. Anyone who knew my mum loved her, she was wise and thoughtful, kind, clever and funny, and sometimes brutally honest. She had always told my brother and I that she would willingly have died with our father. They were an absolute love match and she never sought to replace him. Her one focus after he died was us, she stayed for us. So now in her eighties with a strong faith she was more than willing to go and be with my dad. A nurse herself she had no fear of dying but only wished to die well. She had stayed alive this long not because she particularly wanted to but because a six-year-old boy, and a four-year-old girl needed her to. She stood up, held firm and was an inspiration to us both.

Leukaemia was her ticket to my father, and she was genuinely relieved to be going; what none of us banked on was her tenacity.

"I will be dead by Tuesday, won't I?"

"Anne has to go to Spain on Tuesday I must be dead by then."

Every day in the hospice, until she drifted into unconsciousness, she pleaded with the staff for it to be over. She knew the sacrifices myself and the family had made, she had said her goodbyes and was ready, but cruelly we waited ten long days. I do believe I was watched closely by the staff, as there may have been suspicions, I would finish her off in order to board the plane. True to her word, she died in my arms with Hello Dolly blaring out her favourite song. With the smallest of smiles on her face after ten long, pointless days and nights in the hospice it was over. Three days later I was lying by the pool, in the safety and love of my besties I had met that first day at Epsom (picture 10).

When you are told you're going to die it is inevitable to want to know how long. It is the impossible question, because nobody knows. You can be told an approximation, based on averages for your particular disease, and your condition, but it's basically just guesswork. I do believe there was a case in our hospital of a patient being told they had a very short time to live so they set about ordering their life. Houses were sold, bucket lists were ticked off, but he failed to die. Now homeless and destitute he sued the hospital.

If a loved one dies too soon and earlier than anticipated those left behind feel cheated and deprived of valuable time. Maybe a wedding was brought forward but not soon enough, and occasions were missed and can never be replaced. Or like me, you take on all the care for a loved one. Thinking you can manage your ward of one, single-handedly, twenty-four seven, only to be stretched too thin and suffer and falter yourself.

Using time wisely is key, and something I always tried to relate to my cancer patients. Facing the reality that it is inevitable, but that they have choices. There is help and support that you can access making those final weeks or months more bearable. In my experience the better the acceptance and preparation for death, the less traumatic and swifter the grieving process.

I didn't return to work, the toll on me had to be paid and I concentrated on my husband and daughter and used the time and peace to heal myself. Never knowingly idle I built a fabulous shed, come small house at the top of my garden. It was something I had long hankered to do and with my brother, power tools and hard labour I think it was a very effective tonic to grief. Sharing it with him, I think, was priceless in healing us both.

I started a craft business and wrote a book. I didn't appreciate it at the time, but one of my mother's friends said after she had read it, that it was about my parents, their personalities and their love. Six months away from nursing and I was ready to return. I applied for, and held the role of pancreatic cancer nurse specialist for a year after my mother died. It was an intense job, hugely demanding and with good old hindsight on my side now, it was probably too much, too soon.

I remember sitting at my desk, having missed calls from my daughter, listening to an answer-phone message asking "Are any of my parents coming home tonight?" My husband had always had a very demanding and responsible job some distance from home so was always gone before we woke up and home late. This was the slap in the face I needed to concentrate my energies on my daughter, I could literally hear my mother telling me off. In her mind, and mine, no job is more important than how you parent.

It was a lesson well learnt. Taking on a job in cancer you need to be resilient and to have dealt with your own grief before you should try and support others. The prognosis from pancreatic cancer is very poor, and although I enjoyed the rewards from helping others it eroded my fragile recovery and it was a good time to leave.

A couple of years passed and we had got through A-levels with my daughter, she was about to fly the nest. I find the current student loan system abhorrent and immoral, so decided to fund as much as possible of the next steps of her education myself. It sounds very noble when I write it, but there was another less virtuous motivation. The real spur to get me back into the NHS was a letter from the pensions department. If I didn't return to the NHS within the next year the pension, I had always paid into would change automatically to the new pension scheme. Faced in my forties with being cheated out of my pension was a huge incentive to work again.

Despite numerous attempts to change it over the decades, with bribes and lies to the 'new and improved' pension, I held fast. The index linked;

final salary pension was universally known to be one of the best. Most importantly I could take it aged 55 but I had to work again for the NHS to secure it.

They tried to change our pension when we were still student nurses, but we were wily enough to know these changes would never in our best interests, and should always be declined. I count myself as extremely lucky to be able to be retired in my mid fifties, it is as it should be, and I am relieved. To work into my sixties when I probably will have new knees and an even worse back courtesy of my career, would not be a viable option.

So often in life I find things have a way of working out. Seated under my gazebo with my partner in crafty crime Jill, along came the lady who coordinated the UGI (Upper Gastro Intestinal – top end of the digestive system) MDT (Multi-Disciplinary Team). Every cancer has an MDT office with a team of clerical, nursing and doctors. In order to meet waiting times, deadlines and ensure cancers are diagnosed and treated in a timely manner, these teams meet weekly with all the other medical experts concerned. The radiologists who decipher the scans and the oncologists who prescribe chemotherapy and radiotherapy. Along with the doctors who name the cancer under a microscope and the doctors and surgeons who try to treat it.

I should say after leaving the pancreatic cancer job I did pop back to cover this service after a phone call from the head doctor. The only nurse covering pancreatic, stomach and oesophageal cancer was on long term sick with stress. I had worked as part of the team when I was a pancreatic cancer nurse and really the only who knew it. The plan was always to temporarily cover the work until the resident nurse returned or they could recruit a new one. I was able to cover the pancreatic side and the upper GI nurse roles and had been offered a permanent job then, but had declined it for work life balance. Now here I was a year after my temporary stint, thinking a couple of days a week in that role would secure my pension and fill my daughter's universities coffers.

And then along came Lyn! Having worked with her before she had come to find me at the market as their part-time nurse specialist had just resigned. They were putting out an advert for an oesophageal and stomach cancer nurse, was I interested. Not that the interview was rigged, as I was the only candidate with appropriate experience, not to mention my experience in research and endoscopy. But when all three interviewers hug you as you enter the room, it usually suggests you have the job. For the next seven years I put all my efforts into that role.

People would often ask how do you do that job? I think the secret in doing an emotionally draining and distressing job is good compartmentalisation. One of the best pieces of advice I have had, and stands true for all nursing jobs; is that you have your own grief and pain, you never need to bring home other people's. Empathy and sympathy are credible and vital components to any nurse, but the art is leaving it at work.

I am sure it isn't universally the case but when dealing with other people's grief it is easier to walk away at the end of the shift if you have already been there, done that, and have your own couple of T-shirts.

The key is focusing on the job, concentrating on how you, in that moment, can help as someone else's world comes crashing down. How can you make it better, easier and less traumatic? You can't change the diagnosis; you can't change the outcome. This is lesson one. In grief, denial must lead to acceptance, and as a cancer nurse you have to be a realist, your aim is to guide and support along this bumpy road. You have to be the helping hand to assist the patient and their family to a place of acceptance. Acceptance that this is true, and real, there is no miracle cure, and this is their fate.

Whether that patient or relative needs to be angry, vent their frustrations and scream at you, that is all fine. Now with Dr Google, all manner of things are promised and nothing usually is true; they may demand treatments and cures that simply don't work. It is their desperation to change course, and gently, but firmly you help them navigate the journey. But you do not carry the angry email home, the formal patient complaints or literally spitting abuse in your face, you leave that all work.

How can you? The answer is simple, it is because you understand what fuels it. There is fear and anger, which is quite natural and nothing, often, that has anything to do with you, or how you have cared for them.

One case that tested this theory to the limit was a patient, whose name on an answer-phone soured the stomach and took every ounce of professionalism to deal with. I had met her and her husband in clinic when she was told she had oesophageal cancer. Her husband throughout our dealings was quiet, patient and calm. I will call her Kim; and she was the opposite. Having many chronic conditions, she stated matter-of-factly she couldn't have cancer because it was too unfair. Her denial lasted for weeks, she called into question the credibility of all the medical staff involved and asked for second opinions on her scans and her biopsies.

The first few weeks were dominated by almost daily abusive phone calls. For a self-confessed, active Christian lady I actually had to call her husband to check if this behaviour was consistent and normal for her. (Occasionally cancer will spread to the brain and patients exhibiting personality changes should always be investigated).

As is usual with this form of cancer, three months of gruelling chemotherapy is undertaken prior to major surgery. So came the time for lengthy emails and calls demanding the oncologists and surgeons look into alternative therapies. Hyperbaric chambers and high-dose oxygen, were combined with cancer killing diet plans, and as long as they didn't interfere with her chemotherapy the team were happy for her to continue.

Kim never warmed to the team, constantly berating and complaining about us. So much so, we often joked in the office she was a secret patient sent to check our responses, push us to our limits and the service we gave. Sent as an experiment to try and break us.

Then came the day of her major surgery. Part of our service was to meet the patient and close family and wait with them prior to going into the operating theatre. An esophagectomy is an all-day affair for two surgeons and never undertaken lightly. For patients and families, it is quite rightly a very daunting prospect. Once the bubbly theatre staff had whisked off the patient it gave an opportunity to reassure and inform the family of what comes next. Pre-Covid that meant showing them intensive care and explaining what they could expect to see when they next saw their loved ones after the surgery.

It was a tiny part of the role, but I loved it, and the morning of Kim's surgery I had to take some deep breaths, and 'gird my loins'. On form she was vile, rude to the surgeon, rude to her husband and rude to me. Her poor long-suffering husband apologised, over, and over again as I walked him round to ITU.

My next shift came, and so too, my other obligation to Kim. Again, not something I, in any way, wanted to do, was to visit her on the ward. I had been off for a few days and she had flown through ITU and was now on surgical high care. (a ward specialising in major surgery, a halfway house from ITU and a normal ward) As I approached, the curtains were pulled around her bed space and I can remember thinking, maybe I can give it a miss.

But that's nursing folks, in a nutshell! You have to do the shitty jobs, even when you're not in the mood. Peering through the gap, Kim was sat up in the bed obviously having washed herself. Washing is a loose term nowadays in hospital with a tiny cardboard bowl and some wet wipes; but don't get me started on this basic failing.

"Oh Anne, how lovely to see you, come in, come in." She reached out and held by hands. I waited, waited for the complaints, but there were none, she was pleasant, most unusually nice even, and thankful, I was very confused.

At our weekly MDT meeting every new patient is discussed, scans checked and results verified, as care is planned by a committee not a lone Doctor. Kim had a mention that week, with one surgeon asking the surgeon who operated on her if he had slipped and done a lobotomy (removed part of the brain, an old treatment for insanity), as the patient in bed six of surgical high care bore no resemblance to the one we had all got to know, and not love, over the preceding four months.

Kim went from strength to strength and recovered well from her surgery. For three years we all waited for the bubble to burst but she remained a lovely lady. In follow-up clinic, not only did she no longer scream at you, but there were home-made cupcakes and crushing hugs. Experiencing this monumental effect on an otherwise delightful lady was the epitome of what fear can look like, presenting itself as outright anger and rage.

Kim also taught me another huge lesson. I had been on leave and my colleague told me Kim and her husband were in our little consultation room. Without stopping to hear why, I trotted in to claim my hug and a catch up. She looked pale and had lost a little weight, which she was telling me all about when one of our surgeons walked in. I sat and listened as he told them sadly, her recent CT had shown the cancer was back, and it had spread everywhere. This tragically is not unusual, the bastard cancer lays dormant, and after putting patients through the hell of chemotherapy and major surgery, and then often chemotherapy again, it comes back to get them. Patients are like children, a good nurse shouldn't have favourites, but when you spend years getting to know them, you just do; and Kim had become one of mine.

When you give a patient terrible news you usually first suspect it yourself, order tests, have the ability and necessity to know that diagnosis in advance of the patient. It is vital to best arrange how, by whom and when, to impart that cruel news and to emotionally and psychologically prepare yourself for that conversation. With all that said, I would still cry with my patients. They were not strangers, but trusted medical friends. It is very different to tell a perfect stranger bad news, but recurrence in the surgical patient is the most harrowing on the team, and of course the patient and their family.

There on the sofa with Kim and her husband, I had been denied the pre-warning and unwittingly had not applied my professional cape that protects and allows us to do the job. The news hit me as if I were family, it is one thing to sniff back tears and get on with the job in hand, but that day I sobbed.

I hadn't realised until that day how well I protect myself, until my guard was down and I was vulnerable. There is no university module or competency you can be signed off for, to prepare anyone for this. It is a skill, a layer of professionalism which is hard to quantify; and that day I felt the full weight of it not being there.

Photos 8 to 16

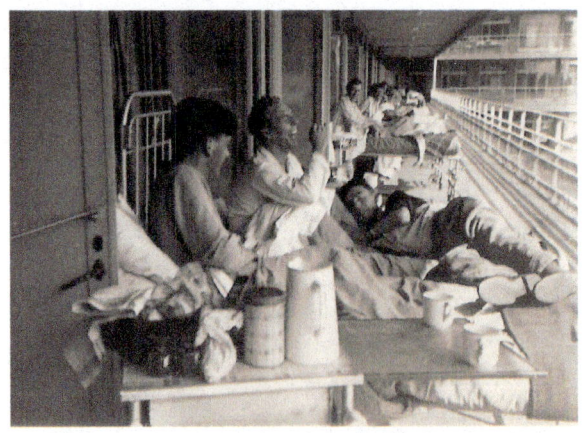

Photo 8 – Broomfield Sanatorium, Chelmsford. My Dad's home for two years as a patient.

Photo 9 – My home for three years during training (Epsom Nurses Home)

Photo 10 – The Feb '86 Gang goes to Marbella 2011, to celebrate 25 years of nursing together. Love you "ladies".

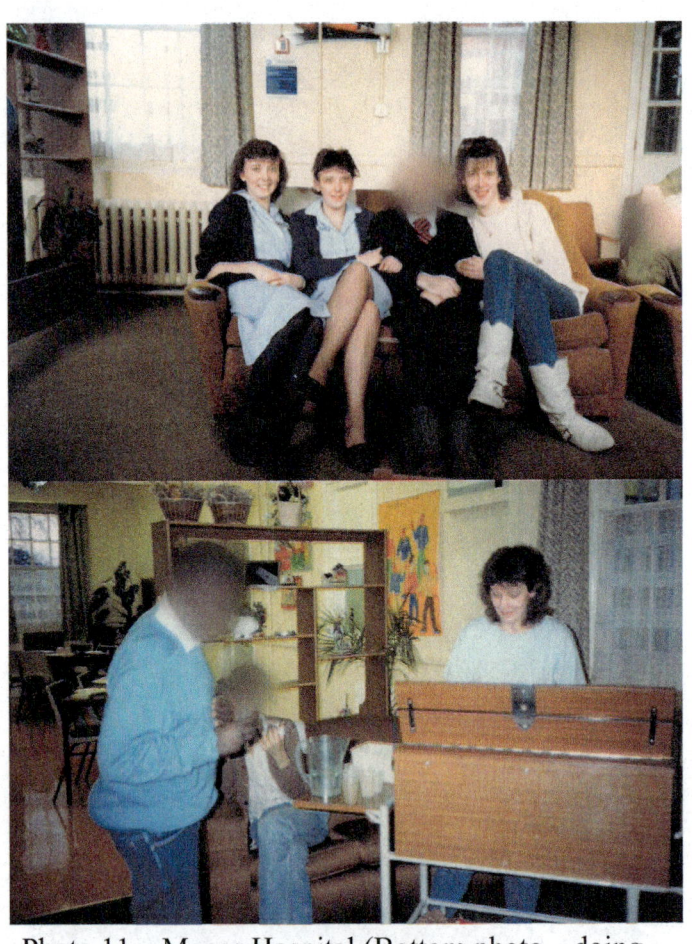

Photo 11 – Manor Hospital (Bottom photo – doing the drug round in my jeans)

Photo 12 – Thank you to the surgeons who bought a menopausal woman's best friend – a fan you can work through.

Photo 13 – The SPLASH Support Group committee members, my patients, my friends (at my retirement do).

A surgical award recognising awesomeness for Anne who helped keep the UGI CNS service running during the pandemic

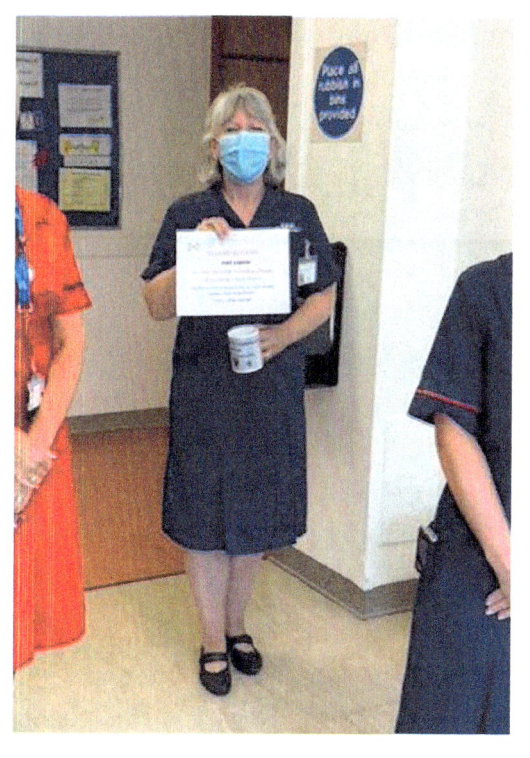

Photo 14 – The award (mug) for 'Awesomeness displayed during a modern pandemic' goes to ……

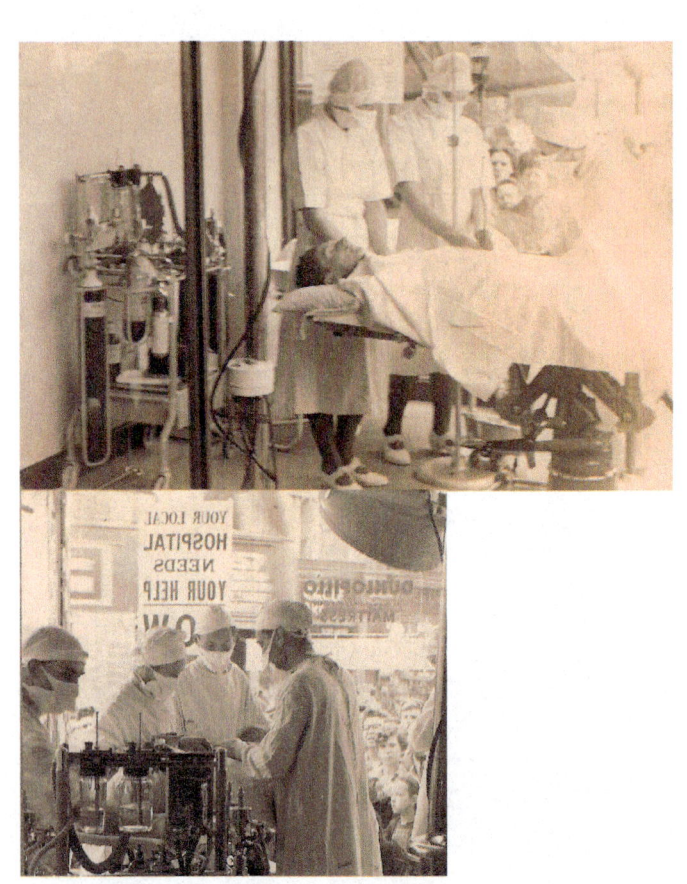

Photo 15 – "Your local hospital needs your help NOW!". A display in a London shop window advertising the "New" NHS. My Dad playing the patient and being operated on in the shop window.

Photo 16 – RGN qualification presentation day, received from the Mayor of Epsom (Note – no cap and gown required).

Perks

There are very few perks to being a nurse, unless you count varicose veins, worn out hips and knees and a completely rogered back. You are surrounded by nurses and doctors, who you can cherry pick to tap for advice, saving on a GP visit, which are becoming increasingly hard to come by. Because you know the system and the right things to say, can navigate your way through if you or yours have an illness. Twenty years apart I have twice had infected in growing toenails, both removed at the end of the shift by willing surgeons who enjoy the practice.

Much more likely, and not really a perk, you will be the go-to person for friends, neighbours, family, friends of neighbours, families and so on. When pressures of the NHS, and gaps in care need filling, you will be in demand. Whether it is to dress wounds, look at a rash or give injections you will be wanted.

Being a student nurse has its perks, even being an old nurse meant I could shop early in Waitrose during Covid. But in my youth, I must admit to having stayed in uniform to drop off or collect my car from the garage as there was often a level of pity, and at least the hope that you weren't going to be ripped off. We were pretty young things, not adverse to a party in the doctor's mess or invite to the fireman social night. But my small group of friends started our nurse training boyfriends in tow, and for the most part are still married to them now.

The rule of not having visitors of the opposite sex stay over in your room was left over from when a matron lived in squalor with you. There was no one to police it now and we all upgraded our single beds to double sofa beds. There was a rowdy element in the nurses' home, which often involved a group of Irish nurses who lived on my corridor. To get enough student nurses even then when they paid you to do it, the hospital would recruit in Ireland. A whole set of nurses would come over together and boy did they know how to party. Luckily, I am blessed with a deaf ear so loud songs in the wee small hours in the echoing stairwell didn't disturb me too much. Slamming of two concertina lift doors right next to my room could be ignored but not, unfortunately their favourite trick.

Just for the craic apparently, after copious alcohol it was the height of fun to set off the fire alarm. Original to the building this was a huge red metal bell attached to the wall above the door of my room. It soon became obvious, even this was no guarantee to rouse me as I was such a sound sleeper. My friends would have to run from their rooms to the other end of the building, or from the floor below to make sure I was awake and had exited safely. Of course, the numerous times this happened it was always a false alarm, but we were never going to ignore the call to evacuate. Only then the true extent of how many overnight visitors there were could be seen. As the fire brigade arrived a stream of bleary-eyed nurses exited the building in various states of undress. Running into the shadows were a constant stream of young men hurriedly dressing as they left.

We were on the whole the stereotypical nurses from the carry-on films. A feminist activist nightmare, we wore stockings and suspenders and enjoyed being wolf whistled at. The only time I ever experienced feeling a sense of sexual harassment was on a day trip to Headley Court hospital and even that wasn't wholly unwelcome.

The hospital was nearby and an excited coach-load of student nurses set off. PE bag in hand with shorts, trainers and swimming costumes. The military hospital specialised in the recovery and rehabilitation of injured service personnel. Remembering in the 80s, just as most nurses were female, most soldiers, airman and sailors were red blooded young men.

We were met by a senior officer; I have no idea which service or what rank, but what was abundantly clear was that he was in charge. He told us for this day we were in the services and would do what we were ordered to do, we stood like frightened rabbits and nodded. We all lacked the courage to argue with a ward sister let alone a sergeant major (or whatever he was).

I have always felt safety in numbers and this quelled my nerves as I stood with my friends, what could happen we were all together? This was soon shattered as we were divided up. I was placed with a group of young men with spinal injuries. I envisaged sitting and talking about their ordeal over some macramé or basket weaving, how wrong I was. The first exercise was basketball, I was excited, I had played at school so felt up to the challenge. This, however, was seated basketball, with each player sat on a small Hessian Square. You had to propel yourself using your heels and hands, which I discovered, I was very bad at. The main aim of the game seemed not to score baskets but to throw the ball at the terrified nurse so the opposition would thunder across the hall to get her. I squealed and I turned, and was completely exhausted having travelled only a few feet at the end of the match.

The second activity was outside, and naïvely I admired the grounds expecting I would watch, maybe hold a clipboard as the troops did their thing. The man in charge explained to the group of roughly a dozen men aged 18 to 30 that they now had to run twice around the gardens. The formal lawn sloped down with huge hedges either side, I would have been more than content to wait and watch.

"You, nursey have a five-minute head start." I looked in disbelief, he grinned. "GO!"

I didn't need telling twice. I hurtled down the lawn trying to get distance from the baying whistling pack behind me. Of course they caught me, some even ran little circles around me, there were grabs and pinches and one soldier tried to grab me into a gap in the hedge. I had never been a natural runner and spent all my school days avoiding the activity, but it's surprising what you can accomplish when being chased down by a motivated battalion.

Feeling every inch like the Fox in the hunt, I don't think I've ever ran as fast, and the adrenaline fuelled panic was exhilarating, but never frightening. Relief came with lunch, the services certainly feed their patients better than the NHS. I was exhausted, 'thanks fellas, I've had enough now' apparently wasn't an option. Early afternoon was tailored therapy so I accompanied a young soldier whose vehicle had overturned fracturing his spine. The care these wounded servicemen received was first-class. Had I known I could have trained as a nurse in the military and been saluted by my patients I may well have taken that career path.

I had relaxed and tuned back into why I was here, my headspace firmly in nursing and rehabilitation when the last activity was announced. Swimming, really! I was fit and slim and having grown up by the sea had no qualms stripping off for a dip. I was however regretting the blue stripy bikini, now wishing I had opted for a Victorian bathing suit or even a wetsuit. Much whistling and heckling was rewarded with blushes; but a huge relief that I was a strong swimmer. Again, I was given a head start and the deafening "GET HER!" and my ability to pound out front crawl without taking a breath saw me reach the other end of the pool unsullied.

I remember the coach journey back to the hospital a mixture of exhilaration and humiliation across all of our exhausted faces. The next morning, we made a sad entrance to the classroom as we all hurt in muscles, we didn't know we had, or had yet learnt the names of.

I believe truly the greatest perk of nursing is the camaraderie, I imagine it is similar to being in the forces. That team sprit that pulls you through, the togetherness that supports and gives you the strength in adversity. The spirit of the blitz, that pushes you to keep your head up, smiling when inside you are exhausted and afraid. This bond was formed in your training, three long years together. Another loss to the profession that modern day nurses are denied.

This sisterhood, these ties are the life belt that help carry you through incredibly difficult times. Yet again it is not tangible or auditable and certainly not something you can experience or attain through independent learning. It was firmly embedded during your training, transferable and stayed with you for your whole career. Regardless of the speciality, you are part of a team. Hopefully a well-oiled team, that you can trust with the shared care of your patients. One poor nurse will reflect poorly on the whole team, and in nursing you are only as good as the worst member of your staff.

There must always be a shared and agreed philosophy, a minimum standard to work by and ultimately, patients and their care, must be, the number one priority. This is what makes nursing a vocation and not just a job.

Mental Health

Nowadays the press and all forms of media are littered with people's opinions on their own mental health. When I started nursing there was no such thing as being off sick because of mental health. If you couldn't take the stress and strain of the work, you simply left and went elsewhere. So, for me the term mental health applies purely to working with patients with diagnosed forms of dementia, psychosis or brain injury. I fully appreciate I am no expert but will now impart some of my experiences in that area.

Part of our training was a stint in mental health. Epsom was well supplied with the sort of 'insane asylum' you just don't see anymore. There was West Park and the Manor hospitals that formed part of our training (there were five such hospitals in total) and we were divided up to work on different wards. I was destined for Manor hospital, a sprawling collection of Victorian blocks, housing many patients in rolling grounds. I was very relieved to be placed with Mandi in my group, as I was sure I was not going to enjoy this. I had no understanding, or experience and would gladly have stayed that way. The villa or ward we were assigned to was for 'young men with behavioural problems' the youngest patient was 19 and the eldest was 57 (See Photo 11).

    I have no recollection of learning what syndrome or condition resulted in their incarceration, but I do remember no one visited. In the eight weeks I worked there no family came, no one apart from the staff apparently cared for the inmates. A patient greeted Mandi and I at the door on our first day; he wore a trilby hat and a tweed jacket, apparently, he had dressing up for our arrival. Derek had been admitted as a small boy because he was 'slow' having suffered from epilepsy, he had spent 50 years on this ward. Had Derek been born today he would have functioned very well in assisted living and could probably have held down a little job. But 50 years of being told when to eat, sleep and leave the building minimises a person. The true definition of institutionalisation.

    Now these rambling hospitals are closed and sold off as flats and people like Derek live their best lives in houses with full-time carers and even have their own cars (not that they can ever drive them). My, how times have changed, and in this case mostly for the better.

The only concession the hospital could make in recompense for imprisoning Derek was to allow him his own bedroom. Who knows how many decades that took, but he was secretive and would become very agitated if you tried to enter. The other patients slept in a long communal dormitory. The main doors were locked and the windows barred. The ward sister's office, kitchen and Derek's room opened out onto a large dining room. Room dividers served to break up the enormous room that led into a lounge with sofas, chairs and a TV set. Beyond this were two rows of beds leading to the enormous bathroom; Toilet cubicles with doors that didn't lock and a huge room with two large bath tubs.

Privacy was not available here and the inmates were stripped and dipped. The experience of being involved in this weekly activity is always recalled when seeing sheep dipping; one by one, unwilling with a look of mild terror in their eyes, exactly the same. Some of the patients couldn't communicate at all, the others on a spectrum from there to Derek. The most pitiable was a young man who clutched a Fausty blanket and sucked his thumb. He towered over me, well over 6 feet tall he spent his entire life, every waking moment hopping as if he had springs in his slippers. His inability to be still used whatever energy his food provided and he was emaciated and stick thin. Any attempt to touch or soothe his relentless movements would end in a high screech and he would bounce away.

A fascinating Italian man in his 30s enjoyed the novelty of having student nurses and took it upon himself to follow, order, and remind you of all your duties.

"Nursie, Nursie you do drugs now!"

He had a facial tick and disliked eye contact and was a born organiser. He had a shopping trolley and large striped bag that he carted everywhere. They were obviously heavy and woe betide you if you tried to touch them or look inside; I dread to think what was in there but we never found out.

One late shift, my husband, then boyfriend, drove me into the grounds for my shift. Yet another late shift Saturday followed by an early shift Sunday, oh the joys of being a student. But when you live the opposite side of the M25 this constituted three years courtship as a weekend off was a rarity. As we pulled up in his shiny new Renault 5 the aforementioned patient had been waiting at the door for my shift to start. Some residents were allowed off of the ward, he being one of them. Picture if you can Danny DeVito as the Penguin in Batman, for with numerous layers of clothing padding out his fame the patient marched out in front of the car.

"Nursie you late!"

Frowning through the windscreen he advanced, thumping the bonnet hard he shouted,

"Nursie, you come in!" With a flick of his hand, he glared at my boyfriend, and bellowed whilst pummelling the bonnet of his prized car.

"You, you go, GO!"

The car doors were locked the minute I was out of the car and he sped off down the drive, strangely he never offered to give me a lift to work again.

Mandi and I were fond of that patient and many of the others. One though we never warmed to had no verbal communication and his only hobby appeared to be creeping up on you unexpectedly, and swinging his exceptionally long arms. One drugs round I turned, and got a fist in the stomach that landed me feet up on the sofa and very winded.

The man in charge of the villa was a large Indian charge nurse. I rarely saw him interact with patients/clients/residents (not sure what the PC descriptor is at the moment) At times something would unsettle the atmosphere in the unit. From the usual calm, contentment something could aggravate one or two, and like a forest fire before you knew it, they were all unsettled and agitated. Many of the staff talked about the genuine effect the full moon could have, often generated unease. Lunatic, or Lunny bins as these places were described in my childhood (Yes, I'm well aware that's very un-PC but it is a fact). Were so called because they historically thought to be affected by the moon and its cycles.

  Usually the charge nurse would hear, sensing a change and walk out of his office. The effect was instant, as he walked, they calmed. Mealtimes were regimented and a set order had to be maintained. All the residents sat at their allotted table always in the same chair. The food was delivered in a stainless-steel trolley and the student nurses usually served whilst the charge nurse walked round the tables and told them when to come up for their food with their plate. I had the routine down, my initial anxiety at working here had for the most part gone. I knew who to give a wide birth to, and who would masturbate at me, "I like you nursey!" This patient was overweight and lumbering on his feet and I could outmanoeuvre him. The 'thumper' had a small shuffling gait so I could out run him, as for the rest although they could get agitated, they filled me with no fear. One lunch-time there was an alarm sounding just as our food trolley arrived. I had never seen the charge nurse move so fast as he fled the dining room with calls of;

"There's an incident downstairs I'll lock you in."

Whether it was the alarm, the deserting calming influence that was the charge nurse, or that I was exuding fear from my pores, but a grumble of unrest started to swirl around the room.

"Quiet now, quiet!" I tried for my best authoritative voice.

Table one came up, as did my voice; meaning to be assertive it was tremulous and weak and had zero effect. The silence now was punctuated with mumbles and groans, and the seated residents twitching and fidgeting in their seats. Again, I tried to calm them, but the unrest was rising to agitation. Several were on their feet; the human coiled spring had bounded off to the lounge but many startled eyes were fixated on me.

In line with their rising agitation, they advanced towards me. Pulling the trolley to the corner of the room with no shame but a large dose of fear I equipped myself with the fish slice and a ladle. Arms outstretched and waving wildly my overriding aim was to leave the shift alive and unabused. Thankfully, stainless steel utensils are a deterrent and no one was injured on that day. Needless to say, as soon as the charge nurse returned normal service resumed and I used the implements for their intended purpose.

The villa we were assigned to was not for the 'dangerous patients' per se, but whilst on our placement we visited two other wards. The first was tragic. In a large ward that had once been open plan, attempts had been made to segregate private areas; a single bed, armchair, bookcases and lamps and in every area sat, vacant looking old ladies. The relics of a bygone days and testament to the misuse of these institutions. When you could be 'locked away' for offences, ranging from teen pregnancy to stealing a bicycle. These were the forgotten convicts with no diagnosed mental health issues but were guilty of being wilful, headstrong or just caught up to no good. A social experiment proving that imprisoning someone long enough and telling them they are crazy can and will sap the soul of a person. So damaged they could never be reintroduced to normal life and condemned to live out their days waiting for death to release them.

The other area we visited was a female locked ward. Mandi and I entered the first locked door, waited until it was locked behind us before the second one was unbolted. These residents could never leave the ward like some of our patients did. We stood in a large spacious area with a few patients slowly pacing and the staff watching them cautiously.

"Don't engage with anyone and stay near me." The strong male nurse didn't need to give us this advice and I would willingly have clung to his back. We were shown the padded room, yes, they really did exist (at least in the 80s). One patient was screaming and pounding the walls and hitting her head against the stained padding of her room. I would happily have turned tail and ran, but Mandi's eye was caught by a fragile looking young girl edging over to us. She had large eyes and an elfin beauty and seemed quite incongruous in this setting.

"Be nice… Be nice!" The nurse repeated as she grew nearer. In my confusion I thought he was talking to us, but this all came clear when she launched herself screaming and spitting towards Mandi. The thin gold chain ripped from her neck leaving long red scratches where it had once lain. Two nurses sprang from their seats and dragged the girl away kicking and biting.

"Can we go back to our ward now please?" If nothing else Mandi and I felt suddenly, inexplicably safe back in our villa with our band of young men. Those who could function and enjoy the experience we took to the zoo and into town. Some enjoyed swimming and I, the person who never passed up the opportunity to swim, volunteered to accompany them - only the once! The pool was of dubious cleanliness and the water, whether it was psychological or not, had a texture. It had a disconcerting, glutinous, more than liquid feel to it. A diluted wallpaper paste feel, that made me imagine I was immersed in a pool of snot, or even more worrying solid particles.

I've swum in harbours with crabs, and beaches with dubious cleanliness but never have I held by head so high from the water. As my few patients splashed and enjoyed their time with their armbands and rings, my goal was obviously to keep them afloat. Equally though, to keep the water off my face and from any possibility of ingestion. I was extremely relieved for the visit to the locked ward and Mandi's incident or I would never have known to swim faster than the pretty blonde teenager who stalked me around the pool in an oversized rubber ring. A few times when paying attention to my patients she would get too close and I could push off from her inflatable and swim to safety.

You certainly learn along your journey through nursing where your skills lie, what you enjoy and what you loathe. Mental health is rights on top, number one in the loathe pile. After my eight weeks I've vowed never again to voluntarily put myself in that environment.

I completed my training and I joined an agency. A crisp white agency uniform, hair neatly pinned up and a fresh-faced newly qualified nurse at your service. It takes a very special nurse to work for an agency, yes, the wages are better but where you will be sent and what you will be expected to do is not always worth the financial reward. For the next little anecdote suspend disbelief because I write a true and accurate account of the most terrifying night of my life.

For those who can remember the world pre–Sat Nav it was a daunting task driving somewhere new. I was absent the day they handed out a sense of direction and on a cold stormy night I drove down country lanes horribly lost in the Cheshire countryside. Having only moved north a few months before, I am amazed to this day I ever did find it. But by the time I found the locked high gates I was on the point of turning around and giving up on this particular night shift.

"You just have to look after a single lady in her home", they said, it will be fine, they said.

A storm was raging, and the intercom in the gate connected and the response I had, should have made me turn around in my beetle and drive home. But I'm a professional, so when the female voice screamed back at me to get my 'bloody arse inside now' I foolishly followed the drive up to the large house. The house itself was imposing and impressive, more like a large nursing home or stately home than any individual's residence I had ever been in.

The patient's daughter unbolted the front door and barked orders at me. She was a very important person apparently, who was late for a very important business meeting in London, and I was the stupid girl who had made her late. I was there to look after her mother who had dementia, I hoped the Apple had fallen a long way from the tree and I was set for a night with a pleasant old lady. I was ushered into the kitchen and shown the box of medicines.

"Give her these as instructed, my numbers are by the phone and the housekeeper will come and let you out in the morning."

Off she stormed in a flurry of indignation and superiority. The key message I had yet failed to appreciate was 'let you out'. My patient was to be found in the lounge apparently and all I had to do was help her to bed, give her the medicines and be there. I made my way through the enormous hall with its carved oak staircase turning up and around, antique furniture littered with expensive ornaments and silver picture frames. The applause echoed from the far door which I assumed was from the television.

Sitting in the vast lounge opposite an enormous inglenook fireplace was a small lady, eyes firmly fixed on Blind Date.

"Good evening, my name is Anne, I'm your nurse for this evening." Smiling my best caring smile she slowly looked over. Her banal expression landed on me and I smiled harder, her eyes squinted and she rose slowly from the sofa. She was a neat trim little lady in a polyester dress and tartan slippers. After an uncomfortable silence, my forced grin still in place, said lady started shouting. More of a scream really, spittle spraying as she advanced.

"You are a whore, I'm going to kill you! You whore, you slag!"

Bemused more than afraid I remember saying.

"No, I'm a nurse"

Somewhere in this addled mind maybe the three things were symbiotic. It soon became apparent that there would be no reasoning with her and I decided to retreat and maybe start afresh. Back in the kitchen I placed the medicines in to a mug, seeing now that there were enough anti-psychotics and sedatives to fell a horse. Priority number one was obviously to get these down her. My second entrance to the lounge was equally unsuccessful and I was chased into the hall. She was surprisingly spry and agile, but I narrowly escaped by hiding in the under stairs cupboard. Wedging the door shut I waited until the muttering and footsteps receded and peering through the crack of the door, I could see she was once again on the sofa.

I was, to say the least, very confused. As mentioned previously, mental health is not an area about which I am knowledgeable, or at all, a willing participant. Tiptoeing into the kitchen I barricaded myself in by pushing the table in front of the door. I had noticed there were metal bars at the windows and trying the back door, the sinking awareness took over, that I was in fact locked in. I searched for the keys, to no avail, I crept back across the hall to find the front door locked with no means of escape. Creeping back to the kitchen I called the phone number of the daughter who had run away hours ago.

"That is what I am paying for! Of course she is aggressive, it's her dementia and yes you are locked in the house, the housekeeper will let you out in the morning."

Having only just qualified I knew I would jeopardise my place on the register if I just abandoned the patient; but that thought was balanced with my own safety. Suddenly the threat level rose, no amount of money seemed appropriate and all I wanted to do was run home. But it was eight hours until I would be released so had nothing to do but make the best of it. The following hours saw me following, hiding and occasionally trying to interact. All efforts failed and as the storm raged outside so my unease and mild Terror mounted.

Meanwhile the old girl showed no signs of tiredness or desire to make her way up to her bedroom. I decided to get acquainted with the house and wandered upstairs. There was a large wooden arm that dropped and blocked the 10 feet wide staircase. Easy enough to climb over, or under, but obviously enough of a deterrent to keep her upstairs. Closing it behind me in case she followed, I checked out the layout. A life-size portrait hung on the landing, a study in oil of the lady in question and my least favourite Prime Minister. Whether they were related or friends it did little for my raising stress having their eyes follow my quiet investigations.

    Having found the bedroom I was relieved that it had two entrances, one via the enormous en suite and one via a large dressing room. Ensuring both doors locked from the outside I hatched a plan. It was gone 2am and she was showing no signs of flagging, I had hoped she would nod off on the sofa. Sadly, the pacing and muttering continued, only livened up by outbursts of swearing and snarling when she caught sight of me. She had the unnerving habit of picking up objects such as expensive silver photo frames and blue and white vases. In my agitated mind I was terrified she would hide or break them and I would have to deal with the demonic daughter who would ultimately blame me.

Climbing the stairs and lifting the wooden bar I summons my beleaguered courage and called, (why I did it to this day I don't know), but adopting a child's voice I called out.

"Help, help me."

It worked and the blue floral dress emerged into the hall. I was pleased with my cunning plan because for the first time she sounded rational and even kind.

"Where are you?"

I dare not let her see me as I would just be the 'fucking whore' again. I spoke quietly and she followed my voice up the stairs, across the landing, into the dressing room. She was behind me and I looked over my shoulder, she snarled as I entered the bedroom with her in hot pursuit. As she entered I ran out, across the bedroom and out through the en suite, swiftly locking the bathroom door and then the dressing room door. Hands trembling and heart pounding, at least now there was containment.

"Bedtime now"

I said as assertively and kindly as I could muster, in the hope she would lay on her bed and go to sleep. But now, obviously seeing me for the trampy whore I was she broke into a charge and was beating on the door. I sat with my back against the door and allowed myself to cry. Her tirade of obscenities continued until finally I heard her shuffling away. I was absolutely convinced if she had got to me, she would have tried to kill me. You see films with mad women locked in attics, one of my favourites being Jane Eyre but whenever I watch them, I remember experiencing it first hand.

Despite it being the middle of the night, I returned to the kitchen and called my husband. I sobbed and cried and needed his voice as a comfort, an embrace in my night of terror. He offered to come and get me, but I was locked in. Just knowing I could call him back was a great comfort. I made a large cup of tea and tried my best to get through the night.

I've always known I'm not a brave person and this night certainly reinforced that. If I had wanted, or needed, more tension I would have made up the storm but the thunder and lightning were real. It had every nuance of a nightmare and even though I had secured my raging patient I shook with fear and shock. Never since have I found enjoyment in a horror film.

Having located the nurses' room, I spent the next few hours reading their nursing notes. Usually, a team of two mental health trained nurses would be on duty day and night, and were employed and lived in this room. Four nurses in total lived and managed this lady and yet here was I, alone, a self-confessed hater of mental illness, qualified all of two months entirely out of my depth.

I peered in on my charge who had finally collapsed on her bed, fully clothed but breathing. There was no way I would risk waking her to give her any medication and quite frankly I didn't care that she wasn't undressed and who knows if she'd gone to the bathroom. I had one goal that awful night, to get out as soon as possible. My husband arrived at six thirty and for an hour before the housekeeper came to let me out, I sat in the hall with my fingers through the bars that covered the letterbox and he sat outside holding them fast.

When the housekeeper finally arrived, she insisted that we go upstairs and check on the lady of the house. She lay there snoring, her dress wet with urine and I didn't care. All I cared about was that the sun shone and I was able to escape. I would, and probably should, have felt a level of guilt, had the housekeeper not repeatedly said.

"You poor girl, they should never have sent you on your own. Poor you, there, there there, don't cry."

Laying in a hot bath at home to try and counter the incessant shaking and feeling of ice in my blood, I phoned the agency and resigned. There endeth my foray into mental health. It was many years, and with a much-grown confidence before I attempted agency work again. Of course, there have been patients with confusion and dementia, especially for the time I worked in nursing homes. But none since that night in Cheshire, even come close to what I felt of real madness and terror.

There was a retired fashion designer who lived in the attic room of a nursing home where I was once matron. Having had a stroke, she could neither speak nor stand. She had never married or had children and had no relatives that we were aware of. I witnessed her hundredth birthday and even arranged a telegram from the Queen. The local newspaper came, there was a big cake and balloons all of which she sneered through. I enjoyed the challenge of trying to win her over, drown her with kindness and tenderness; but every day I would wash her and dress her until the crucial moment of wrapping my arms around her waist and pulling her into a hug to pivot her onto the commode or her chair. With a good arm around my shoulder, she would dig in the manicured nails I had painted and sink her teeth into my neck. Rather than be upset or angry I would laugh, seat her quickly down, and vow in my dotage to behave exactly the same way.

After relocating back to Portsmouth I spent a couple of years working in nursing homes. The first located by the sea was a patched up, converted Victorian house. Owned by a company in London its employees and boss had no medical knowledge and whose only interest was visiting once a month to collect the fees. The decor was shabby, the furniture battered and the carpets all had an aroma of dirt and urine. It had very little in its favour except the most important thing, it felt like home. The cook was basic but generous and knew every resident's preference. The cleaner was the campest, most crude man I have ever met and the residents loved him. All of the staff were locals and the unwritten ethos was, treat the residents as if they were your nan or mum. I did drug rounds in my slippers, and spent afternoons perched on a little stool painting their nails. I was on first name basis with all the families who were always warmly welcomed.

We worked well as a team and I thoroughly enjoyed being the matron, the hardest part was the lack of investment and interest from the owners. I was lured away by a neighbouring home with promises of better standards and opportunities. The next role really soured my time in nursing homes. These owners had previously been hoteliers and therein lay the problem. This business was all about the look and the profit. Beautiful pink velvet chairs in the lounge and not a whiff of wee, because if you were a messy eater or incontinent you stayed in your room. Gone were personalised treats for residents, the kitchen was locked between meals. If a resident wanted a slice of toast, or cup of tea in the night, that was just tough.

The moral of this story is if you are looking for a residential or nursing home ask the relatives of those there and look past the décor. The sad truth is residents with frequent visitors will get better care. Without doubt a patient with the son in America and a daughter in Australia will have the poky room in the attic with no view. No special care will be taken about laundering their clothes, or enriching their lives. It is also always worth unannounced visits to keep standards high.

Being a CNS

The months since I retired, I have been honoured to help a dear friend through her brave battle with the disease. The last decade of my working life had been dominated by cancer. As previously mentioned, nursing my mother through leukaemia and being the recipient of care from the hospital and hospice started the journey.

Being a clinical nurse specialist (CNS) in cancer was the pinnacle of my career. At times so incredibly hard, but the rewards could be immense. A third of my working life revolved around a weekly MDT (multidisciplinary team) meeting, a cancer weekly clinic and the constant spinning of plates that being a CNS involves. Based in an overcrowded, cramped, excessively hot office the daily routine of 'fire-fighting' patients' issues repeated itself. Two phone lines and a mobile phone, also the constant drip of emails made for relentless days. There was never five minutes when some poor patient wasn't waiting for you to help (See Photo 12).

Some cancer specialisms are split between curative and palliative; the first is obvious and the latter means although there may be treatments to slow the cancer there is no cure. Within oesophageal and stomach cancer, my chosen branch, there was deemed no funding or requirement for a palliative cancer nurse specialist. Myself and my fellow CNS and a small merry band in the office were funded from a surgical budget. The role was created by surgeons and we existed to manage the pathway and support the patient and families of those who could be offered potentially life-saving surgery.

We were consistently deaf to the statements of, 'You are not paid to look after the dying ones". Or, 'They are with oncology now we don't need to worry about them', which were levelled at us when we complained we were stretched too thin. Of course, once we got to know a patient and more importantly, they had our number, they could, and would always call us.

It should never be in a nurse's vocabulary to say 'Sorry that's not my job.' People are your job and if anyone is asking for help it is your duty to help. Whether that is to contact the correct department and ensure they are aware, or help them yourself, you should always endeavour to do your best. My toes always curl and my teeth grind, at hearing any nurse utter the blasphemous phrase, 'Sorry not my patient'. If you are a nurse reading this, and you admit to yourself this is something you have been guilty of, wash out your mouth, say some Hail Mary's and endeavour to do better and promise me you will buck up.

A phone call from a palliative patient who has uncontrolled pain, distraught with fear of dying, or with a host of questions, has as much right to a friendly someone they can call as every other patient. It was often inconvenient and time consuming, but I wouldn't have had it any other way. I am delighted to hear since I left, they are now finding the funds, or at least getting a charity to fund a designated UGI palliative care nurse.

One of the most rewarding aspects of the job for me came from the first phone call. The aim was to make first contact with a patient as soon as possible after they had been notified there was a potential cancer. The nature of the beast meant; these cancers were usually found at an endoscopy. People tend to think your insides are grotty places to visit, but this is far from true. Your oesophagus or gullet, stomach and even your bowels with the aid of a little laxative are pink and velvety. When the camera is passed it is usually blatantly obvious that there is a cancer there.

Some very lucky patients will have such an early cancer that it is not obvious to the naked eye, only when the biopsies come back is anyone aware of the cancer lurking there. But for the majority, visually it is usually a foregone conclusion that it is cancer. Once the patient is sufficiently awake and their family member has been called in, they are usually told that it looks very suspicious for cancer. Then the waiting starts. Biopsies routinely take ten days to give a definitive result and every one of those days the patient waits and worries. Our priority in the office was to contact these patients as soon as possible, the clinicians hopefully informing us on the day of the endoscopy of their findings. We could then book a CT scan within the next week if possible.

These phone calls, which we affectionately called 'cold calling', were often lengthy as a detailed history was taken. It was a crucial opportunity for the patient to ask someone the questions that had deprived them of sleep since their endoscopy. The art is to inform as much as possible, reassure that they will be well looked after, but never give them false hope or lie.

We had two excusable white lies; to questions such as "What does my CT show, is it bad?" It was acceptable, even whilst looking at the computer screen at a truly awful CT scan result, for you to say, "I don't know I haven't seen it, but we will discuss it in MDT and explain it all to you in clinic in the afternoon."

The other alternative of honesty, would be wholly unprofessional. If I had said, "Oh yes, I am looking at it now, and it is terrible, you are riddled." Thus, leaving the patient alone, at home, with catastrophic news, no support or ability to ask questions.

I did once overhear another cancer nurse reply to her patient "I know the results but can't tell you over the phone, you will have to wait for clinic." In my book it shows an arrogance on the nurse's part. It heaps the worry on the patient until they are seen in clinic (because surely, if it was all fine, they would have said) and lastly it breaks the bond of trust. The CNS role is hugely privileged in the depth of personal relationships that are built between the nurse and the patient and family.

Saying something like this would totally undermine that trust and damage that relationship.

Other small ruses were often used, always for the patient's well-being. The patients knew us well enough that if we were calling them in urgently to see a doctor this usually meant very bad news. If I were to phone, they would invariably ask "What is it, Anne? It is bad news isn't it, just tell me." The intention was never to avoid questions or difficult discussions, just to ensure they could be held face-to-face with the appropriate people present. I would have to reassure that all answers will be given later. If the patient pressed the point, I would state I was out of the room when their case was discussed so wouldn't want to speculate and give them false information. Therefore, to prevent this falsehood, our second white lie would be used. Our admin team sitting a foot away from us and well aware of everything that was going on could utilise what we called the 'get out of jail free card'. "Sorry, I am admin and the nurse just asked me to call you and invite you to clinic, I have no idea why."

The initial cold call was your first opportunity to build a relationship with the patient and family. It was often useful to call back when husbands, wives, children or whoever else they needed could be there with them. The ultimate aim was to try and ease their fear, give them confidence that they were in good hands and explain the complex journey upon which they were about to embark. Each week there could be between one and six new patients, every one allotted as much time as they needed.

Once the MDT had discussed the biopsy results and we knew exactly which sort of cancer we were dealing with; and the CT scan had been examined and the extent of the disease known, how far could we see it had spread, a plan was hatched. The patient would be well aware they were being discussed and already had their appointment time confirmed. I think the importance of this initial call cannot be overstated. The difference between meeting a patient in clinic to tell them bad news with whom you have had an hour-long conversation, and those you have never heard or spoken to before, is quite marked. Although not a familiar face, a familiar voice that calls them into meet the doctor when they are utterly terrified is, I'm sure, very welcome.

Obviously, you don't do the job for glory, but it does make it rewarding when the patients would sing your praises in front of the consultants. I was fortunate enough to work with a band of upper GI consultant surgeons, I not only respected but really liked. Where appropriate they all would interject some humour, as would I. On one occasion, during that first clinic appointment, a patient's wife was gushing a little too vociferously about me being a godsend at the end of the phone, when said consultant with a complete deadpan expression and sincere gaze said.

"Yes, we are so lucky to have her, she is so wonderful, but it is a shame she is such a potty mouth."

I laughed so loud, and so hard, I dropped the paperwork I had been struggling to balance on my lap.

For the majority of people once they have had their diagnosis, with some of their fears confirmed, but others dismissed, experience a feeling of great relief. They know exactly where they stand, they have a plan, and hopefully have confidence in the team around them. We always had a sense of failure if we were unable to achieve this. Fear can often present in anger, and aggressive patients and their families were usually won over by the end of the consultation. After the doctor has given them the facts the patient and entourage would follow me (or the other CNS) into an office for a cup of tea and an explanation in layman's terms; probably too many booklets and well-meaning leaflets.

Usually, the tension had dissipated and we could pick up from where the phone call had ended to really get to know them. I have found in nearly all cases humour helps. When all their questions are answered, and I am satisfied that they have understood what is about to happen, a little humour helps them on their way. Leaving them to their grisly task, of having to break the news to family and friends. The outpatient department staff said we were the most cheerful cancer clinic they had, and I was proud of that. It is without doubt, a fine line, and one where it is best tread very carefully; as humour at the cost of empathy and professionalism is disastrous.

Cancer is cruel. The longer our population live, the more inevitable it is that every family will experience it. Cancers are rated from the best to the worst. You really don't want pancreatic, brain or oesophageal. If you had a choice and could pick, you need to go for the ones that are popular and have had the most research and funds. Breast cancer and its treatments have come on incredibly in my lifetime, and survival is much more obtainable. Prostate cancer similarly is eminently treatable these days. I am no oncologist or cancer researcher but it seems to me those cancers that let you know they are there earlier, are more treatable.

Unfortunately, stomach and oesophageal cancer are often ignored and treated as bad indigestion. By the time the gullet is so narrow your food sticks, it has often been there too long to be curable.

Other clinics were not so cheerful, and these were the ones where a medical doctor (gastroenterologist) would have to inform a patient and their loved ones that the cancer was beyond cure. Oncology is the speciality that works with cancer, there is a special place in heaven for doctors who choose to work in this field. These doctors grasp at any new technology and research that can help them prolong a life. But ultimately, as yet, there is no magic bullet for these cancers and the prognosis remains poor. On the brighter side trials are currently underway for a cancer vaccine, specific to one patient's own cancer. Also rolling out are immunotherapy drugs that could radically improve treatment. So hopefully the future is brighter, and these cancers can better be eliminated.

There is one of my patients I will never forget. Brian was the first patient I met on the ward during my first day in the job. Back then, to remove an oesophageal cancer, the patients would have a 'shark bite' incision. A long open cut down their belly and a long cut around their back and side, across their ribs. Recovery from this surgery was very slow and painful, but now, by some form of magic it is all done by keyhole surgery.

Brian suffered with his back wound that just would not heal. He struck me as the nicest of men and over the following weeks I did all I could to help heal his wounds. Frequent clinic visits meant I got to know his lovely wife and daughter well and albeit slowly, he made a full recovery. The team held regular patient support group meetings. These took place on a Saturday where the dietician, nurses, consultants and volunteers would host a couple of informative hours for all the upper GI patients. Friendships were made, buddies found for struggling patients, and a lovely array of cakes provided for everyone. The patient group was more of a family; like most families there were those that didn't want to take part, and those that were the life and soul of the party.

Over the years at these meetings some very strong and genuine ties were forged between the team and the patient cohort. When two thirds of your patients won't make it to surgery, and then a large proportion of those having surgery will be taken by the recurrence of their cancer it can be disheartening for the team. What a tonic to see the ones that have lived on. Knowing their battles through terrible times, yet to come out the other side having fulfilling and active lives makes the job all the more worthwhile. I often thought the meeting was as beneficial for the staff as it was for the patients. Brian and Vera were welcomed regulars.

A few years passed and Brian was very concerned about his brother who had been exhibiting similar symptoms to himself and didn't hesitate in asking for our help. Sadly, his brother was diagnosed with oesophageal cancer but it was too advanced for a cure and he sadly passed away.

Then, a year or so later, Brian called again, concerned about his beautiful wife Vera. She too had the same symptoms, and didn't appear to be being taken seriously by her GP. The team leapt in, and lo and behold she too had the cancer. So, like some awful nightmare, or déjà vu, the family began the cycle of gruelling chemotherapy followed by major surgery. Her recovery was tough and her side-effects challenging, but they never ceased to be a delight to work with.

Another phone call from Brian apologising as he knew it wasn't my job but the family had had yet another blow. Brian's son was relocating back to the area and had just been told he had bowel cancer. Confused and distraught they didn't know where to turn. My office was five doors up from the bowel cancer team, thus I was able to make the connection for Brian's son so that he could get the care he needed.

It must be eight years since I first met Brian and I was devastated to hear that his lovely wife had had recurrence of her cancer and had passed away. People talk about the cruelty of cancer, and how unfair life can be. If ever this was true it is proven by the experiences of this lovely family.

Brian came to my craft market this month with his daughter. There were many hugs and tears, for not only had they buried his lovely wife, he had also lost their son. They were prolific with thanks and praise from my help over the years and I can't convey what that meant to me. It was an absolute privilege to witness a family who fought so courageously, with such grace, always with endless love and support for one another. It was an honour and a pleasure to ease even a tiny piece of their suffering.

Brian read my first novel to Vera near the end as it gave her peace and that is the greatest accolade I will ever receive for my efforts in writing. I contacted Brian's daughter and asked if I could include them in this book. I offered to give them a rough draft to check, to be certain they were happy with it. Her reply was truly humbling, and I think highlights the relationship of trust and affection that can be created through simply doing your job.

"We are happy for you to include the chapter about us. We don't need to read it first as we know whatever you have written will have been done with respect and kindness. Dad sends his best wishes and wants to know where he can buy a copy when it is in print."

Thank you so much Sharon, there it is, what it really means to be a nurse. To know what you did mattered, you hold this dear to your heart and in your memories are the wonderful people you had a small part in helping.

Endoscopy

As I have mentioned before the bulk of my career was spent within the speciality of endoscopy. What started for me in Kent in the early 90s in a one-room theatre with fibre-optic cameras that only a doctor could look down has changed beyond recognition. Nowadays the technology is impressive, the whole team can watch as the camera advances inside a patient on extremely expensive computerised cameras.

In the early days decontamination of the equipment involved hot soapy water and buckets of very dubious cleaning solution. With no concern for the consequences, the whole team could breathe in the fumes of these toxic liquids throughout the day. We were armed with Marigold gloves, and a gung-ho spirit. We were a slightly dysfunctional team of five nurses, but we made the best of it and had fun where we could. A friend had recommended it to me as an option, as I had recently hurt my back when I tried to catch a falling patient in a bathroom, twisting and hearing something go 'ping'. Remembering the heady days before hoists and slide sheets my days in trauma orthopaedics were numbered.

The layout of the endoscopy department was far from ideal and patients waiting for their procedures were uncomfortably far too close to the treatment room. Loud music, even a desperate nurse's singing voice could not always drown out the retching and moaning of patients. One glance at the waiting room could tell you if your efforts had succeeded or failed.

Colonoscopies (passing a metre and a half of camera up your bottom to look at the length of the large bowel) can be really rather uncomfortable. The sister in charge had a technique she utilised and would sit on a stool at the side of the trolley facing the patient who would lay on their left-hand side. She would gently cradle the shoulder with one arm, having the other arm around the patient's head, almost burying their face in her bosom. Constant reassurance and enough sedation and pain relief when needed to make it bearable, combined with her skilfully muffling any moans with her ample breasts was very successful.

One of our consultants suffered with insomnia. He was fundamentally a wonderful man, who was however, cursed with a very short fuse. On my induction day there was a very unfortunate event. It was obviously my fault for not restraining and comforting the patient adequately, as this particular lady was very agitated. Try as I might, but lacking adequate experience and bosom, the patient continued to moan. The needle in her arm which allowed us to give her more sedation was heavily bandaged to a big bulky splint, and she insisted on reaching down with this arm to press on her uncomfortable tummy. The tension was palpable, and the more complicated the bowel to navigate the more agitated the patient and ergo the more annoyed the doctor.

"Get your arm away!"

Quite unprepared was I for what happened next. In one swift movement the patient's arm was lifted and flung off her belly by the irate doctor. In perfect timing I looked up as the heavily bandaged arm slapped me cleanly, square on the forehead. In comedic slow motion I fell backwards, off the stool and flat on my back. Bizarrely it didn't put me off the work, or the doctor come to that. and it somehow cemented our relationship. I loved working with him and did so for many years. I think because of this incident I was spared many of his outbursts.

I have worked with some truly feisty doctors in my time. Only a handful I have genuinely disliked, and the common theme is usually that I distrust their priorities. I can take being shouted at, and have had plenty of things thrown at me. If I know it is born out of concern or frustration for a patient I can and will take it. If, on the other hand I have no respect for them as a doctor, I will let loose my Eastend roots and they will regret messing with me.

I have worked with doctors who I admire and like immensely, and will cut them quite a bit of slack for what would now be seen as bullying or harassment. Our doctors comprise some of the most intelligent people in the country. It does not follow that these gifted, dedicated, fiercely intelligent men and women may not always have the best bedside manner. Old-fashioned I may be (I'm sure you agree) but I want my doctors to be experts, whatever their speciality. If I want hugs and kind words I will look to the nurses and auxiliaries.

I will always stand and defend my patient or fellow staff if I think treatment is unjust, but often, in life-or-death situations this highly intelligent group have no tolerance for mistakes or ignorance. One of my favourites (if I were ill in hospital I would want him to visit) I'm sure will recognise himself if he reads this. Never has a man had such intolerance for numpties.

Chatting to my old colleagues, I understand nurses no longer assist with the most complex of endoscopic procedures in the way we used to. One of the greatest challenges was to assist as the doctor attempted to pass a small tube into the biliary tract (The exit for your bile and pancreatic juices, from your liver, gallbladder and pancreas). Akin to cutting your hair, with the wrong hand, upside down, with thick gloves on, in the mirror - this gives you an idea of the complexity.

It was a partnership of interpreting and predicting what would be asked of you, whilst sweating in a lead apron, having stood for hours with the tension racking up. It involved gripping a syringe filled with dye in one hand whilst controlling the cheese wire knife situated deep within the patient's small bowel with the other hand. This would ultimately cut a small opening in the bowel. Torque and tension often resulted in the minutest of movement of my hands causing too big a movement within the patient.

Instructions were shouted to 'inject dye', 'stop injecting', 'more on the knife' or 'less on the knife'. The nurses' job, to pay very close attention and verbally repeat these commands and do as she was asked. Often these patients were very sick and the risks to their life were real. This certainly was no time for banter or idle chit chat. Many were the times that metres of coiled wire were whipped out of the instrument, resulting in any staff in close proximity being splattered with blood and bile. Resulting in your uniform, hair, face and arms routinely flicked over and speckled in red and yellow

The precision required during this procedure was only matched by the importance to the patient's well-being and diagnosis. On this memorable day, and this particular case, after many hours trying to place a drainage tube the atmosphere was palpable.

"More on the knife!" He bellowed.

"More on the knife" I replied, instruction, repeat, act.

"Not that much, less on the knife!"

I closed the knife by the smallest of movements.

"Too much! MORE ON THE KNIFE!" He was screaming now. Sympathetic glances being shared by all the staff in the room.

"MORE ON THE KNIFE!" He screamed.

My patience had gone, I was spent. I knew in my sweaty shaking state I was close to breaking. Not intentionally or with malice aforethought I replied.

"MORON!"

My inner thoughts had been released, wide eyed worried faces in front of me confirming what I had said. With a slow sideways look his only response was a very small smirk. We continued to work together and I have huge admiration for that man. It was never mentioned again, but always makes the old crowd roar with laughter.

Having spent many years working within endoscopy it was fascinating to watch it grow from what was merely a means of looking inside people, to now the wealth of therapies that can be offered. Now early cancers can be removed which would have previously meant major surgery. Now these patients can go home the same day.

Being a junior sister involved an awful lot of people management. I think if I hadn't been a nurse I would have loved to manage people in any walk of life. As with my love for taking on challenging patients, I equally enjoyed working with some fiery and overly emotional staff. Conflict resolution and fairness were always my main aims. The only downside is when you then have superiors who are poor managers it is a whole other challenge to manage them when they are in charge.

For all the thousands of patients I nursed as they passed through the endoscopy departments, there is one incident in particular I will never forget. This truly was a lesson in what it is to nurse. An inpatient from one of the wards was brought into the department by a third-year student nurse. Laying on the trolley the elderly lady was obviously very confused. When a patient is too confused for whatever reason, to give consent for a procedure a senior clinician must complete a special consent form. This poor, frail lady had no idea why she was with us and clearly didn't want to be there. But a diagnosis was needed as she was losing blood and vomiting blood can never be ignored.

As always, I took the opportunity to impart some wisdom and explain to the student nurse exactly what we were endeavouring to do. I ignored her look of disinterest and rambled on. I also explained, that due to her patient's agitation it would be really comforting if the nurse, a familiar face, would stand within the patient's view and hold her hands. Again, I was given the vacant look and she stood where I pointed but failed to pick up the ladies' hands. I repeated myself, "Please hold your patient's hands". The moment had passed and the procedure had started, and all the student nurse would do was to place two fingers on top of the poor patient's gripped hands. I had my job to do, and so set about reassuring the patient and getting the procedure over and done as soon as possible.

After the procedure I asked the nurse why she had not held her patient's hands.

"I don't know what you mean?"

This was a third-year student nurse. Soon to be qualified and planning care for a ward full of patients. How on earth had she got this far without understanding the concept of holding a hand. I took her aside and gave her a lesson in holding hands. Whatever her reasoning for not doing it, it is not acceptable. One of the greatest gestures you can make to a patient, to comfort, and to reassure them especially during a horrible procedure is to hold their hand. I held her hands in a vice like grip for far longer than she would have liked. The look of distain was obvious, I fear it unlikely she will ever offer her patients that simple gesture of kindness in her career.

Yet again, my fears confirmed that there probably is no module at university on handholding. This is not rocket-science. You have signed up to the caring profession, it goes without saying don't join if you are devoid of compassion and dislike human contact. There should be an innate understanding of communication. Whether it is a small touch or complex conversations these are the main tools of our job. Is this still taught? Or are nurses now too high brow to consider such menial things? A truly sad day for that patient, for me, and for the profession.

The Other "C" Word

To many this is code for a rather unpleasant swearword, to medics it has long been associated with cancer. But now in 2023 no writing about nursing would be complete without discussing the nightmare that was Covid (SARS CoV-2 Virus).

When the news was reporting on the worries of Wuhan, we sat complacently in our office. Before we knew it was even in the country it was apparently in our hospital and about to contaminate us. I was at this time, one of two oesophageal and stomach CNSs, along with a fabulous team providing a service to be truly proud of. As I mentioned before the cancers we worked with are nasty and we were always mindful of recurrence. So, when a patient or relative called in with worries, usually weight loss, lack of appetite, or pain we acted on these concerns.

As a team we were incredibly flexible and ran our own clinics. They were usually overbooked and we were overstretched, but if the patient needed seeing they would be. A distressed daughter contacted us, asking that we would see her father urgently as he had become very poorly. Having recovered from major surgery he was exhibiting classic signs of recurrence of this cancer, so I advised her to bring him to our clinic that afternoon.

He wouldn't eat or drink. I made him a small cup of tea and squatted in front of him, a wizened grey, wretched version of himself with my hands on his bony knees. It was obvious this was no post operative psychological depression; he was a very sick man. Sometimes people need a pep talk, sometimes they need to get things off their chest, and other times they are just ill. He was admitted that evening to a bed on the ward next to our office. My fantastic colleague Tracy had previously worked in intensive care before joining the cancer team. She would go and help to care for this patient because the ward staff, try as they might, could not clear his chest.

Within days my colleague was exhibiting flu-like symptoms and continuously coughing. The office joke was that it was Covid. It is a sad and strange phenomenon that the medical profession can be the most unsympathetic when it comes to each other. I have always been of the mind, that if you are ill, and could give it to someone else, stay at home. But it is surprising that the general ethos of the NHS is just keep going and get on with it. She finally gave in and retreated to her bed and lo and behold, a couple of days later I too came down with the same symptoms.

It was the first time in my life that my whole family was ill at the same time. Usually with a cold or flu one succumbs as another is getting better, the next will then go down. But in this instance, myself, my husband and my daughter spent two weeks in a feverish, breathless stupor. Throughout the day the least affected would have to feed the chickens and the dog, we ourselves lived on water and crackers.

This was before any notified cases had been reported, so, as far as we knew it Covid had not made it to our hospital yet. There were no test strips, there were no PPE and certainly no Thursday night clap.

In our ignorance we battled on with our 'flu', if I had known it was Covid I would have had grave concerns for my husband who was worst affected. It took us months to recover, and months for the coroner to go back in retrospect and examine samples from my lovely patient who had died on the ward in February 2020. He latterly was recognised as the first recorded Covid death in our hospital and we unwittingly had all succumbed. We were not tested, the moment had passed and so started our journey through a global pandemic. Before recounting my experiences, I must honour every person who worked in the caring profession whether it was carers in nursing homes, cleaners, ambulance staff or porters in hospitals up to the consultants. Well done for doing your best, continuing to care and just being there.

We all endured PPE (Personal Protective Equipment), risked our health and that of our families, willing or not, all the while confronted the fear of the unknown. A special mention goes to Ruth. We trained together and she had worked constantly since then. I have checked she's happy for me to say that she enjoyed 30 years in the small private hospital; the equivalent to a gentle mooch around the park in nursing terms. This ending in a private suite at our very own Epsom District Hospital, the only one of us that I know to still be working there.

As elective surgery was suspended the decision to convert this unit into a Covid hub was made. Nurses don't have a choice, a contract will always state you will be moved or relocated anywhere within the hospital to meet the needs of the service. It is not a democracy. It is not put to the vote. You are told, you do it, if you don't want to, you must resign or go off sick.

Ruth went from sitting at a desk, checking blood pressure and talking patients through their pre-op chat, to working in intensive care. During Covid many nurses were redeployed and forced to work in intensive care situations. To say it is a steep learning curve is the mother of all understatements.

Fortunately, being office bound myself, my interactions with my patients were conducted over the phone or standing at the far end of the clinic room. When visiting our inpatients on the wards all I had to don were gloves and a mask. Where possible certain wards were kept 'clean'. Meaning all staff and patients were regularly tested to ensure that they were free of Covid. People still needed emergency surgery, inflamed gallbladders and burst appendix wait for no man. Occasionally I would bring patients into clinic to dress wounds or remove stitches and drains. For this I would add a big plastic apron and a plastic visor on top of my mask. I am not embarrassed, only reasonably pissed off, at being menopausal, and even this level of PPE made my work unbearable. My hands were too sweaty to get the gloves on and the face shield fogged so badly I couldn't see the stitches I was supposed to be cutting.

Nursing someone on a ventilator is a highly technical and skilled speciality, one specially trained nurse to one patient is the norm. During Covid one intensive care nurse would be overseeing 10 patients with three or four totally naive nurses learning on the run.

I spoke to Ruth at the time and have immeasurable respect and awe for her. The ability as a middle-aged woman to work long gruelling shifts in two full layers of PPE alone is commendable. Adapting and learning all that is needed to care safely for the sick patients in intensive care situations is unimaginable. I can only imagine the strength and dedication this took and I applaud you and am humbled by you.

There is a tradition in nursing, that as you age and your knees grind and your back fails from old injuries; the varicose veins are troublesome for standing for too many years so you migrate away from ward work. Office jobs, clinics, and specialist roles that utilise many years of experience are the preferred means of heading to retirement.

Specialists in cancer, pain, diabetes, rheumatoid, inflammatory bowel - the list is endless.

What they all share is decades of experience and the need to not be working on a ward. Outpatient clinics were cancelled, and this cohort of mainly older nurses were used as gap fillers. Thrown into situations leagues out of their comfort zone, most I spoke to were terrified. All had no say in it, and if they protested, they were made to feel useless and inadequate. However, the vast majority rose to the challenge, swallowed their fear, learnt fast, and did what nurses do best – they cared. Not to mention that most of these women were in their menopausal phase of their life where the wrong cotton T-shirt can be unbearable when having a hot flush. I can only imagine two layers of PPE running with sweat, steamed up glasses and a lack of hydration whilst trying to learn complex machinery with menopausal brain fog. It is without doubt, worth a medal of honour.

It is with enormous relief I was spared this. My second Covid hero was Tracy, my boss. Being intensive care trained she was ordered, rather than asked to go back there to work at the height of the pandemic. Your home circumstances don't matter, and she was made to work a hideous shift pattern with no concern for her children at home. Because of her heroism I was needed in my role to keep the UGI cancer service running. We were one, of only a couple of hospitals in the country that was determined to continue operating on our cancer patients. We even had patients move across the country because their hospitals had shut up shop.

These were not normal times, and normal working hours did not apply. My part-time hours soon exceeded full-time, and I voluntarily manned our mobile phone twenty-four-seven. Our patients were still having life-saving surgery, with all the worry and fear that goes along with that, with the spectre of Covid hanging over them. Families could not visit, and so I visited any patients we had daily, reporting directly to their families. Those who were bemoaning lockdown, and having to stay at home had no idea of the hell that was being played out in the hospitals.

I was grateful. Eternally grateful to be allowed to stay and care for my patients, but there was always the threat of being dragged onto any ward to work. I had spent 30 years specialising in endoscopy, teaching, research and cancer and it had been that long since I had worked on a traditional ward. The basics don't change but the technology certainly does, I was very dubious about how much help I would be in a ward full of very sick people. And how safe I would be manning machines that go 'bing' with no idea how they worked.

The hospital was well aware, as was the NHS nationally, that they were asking - no demanding - staff to work out of their safe comfort zones. I along with many others attended up-skilling workshops. The aim was to train us on procedures and equipment with which we were unfamiliar. I spent a long fearful afternoon working through a computer training course on how to keep someone alive on a ventilator. There was always an undercurrent of terror, looking around the room at women just like me. On one such training session, a lovely practice educator I knew from my days in that job, was halfway through showing us the latest syringe driving pumps and how to operate them safely when he threw up his hands and shook his head. Strangely his words of despair were the most comforting to me.

"If we get desperate enough to drag you all onto the wards, I'm afraid you will be shut in a room and used to watch people die".

To me finally, I could see that my skills would be of use. My terror and nightmares that stayed with me for months now eased a little as I could see how I could be of use if the need arose. Unable and unwilling to document observation on a PalmPilot, and with no knowledge of how to use the pumps and array of new equipment I was relieved. I was, at least confident in my fundamental ability to care. I could be shut in a room with a handful of desperately ill people and make them comfortable. Because when medical technology is unable to save these people, I knew, I could offer them some comfort and dignity and hold their hand when their families weren't allowed to. I certainly had the skills to, but luckily for all concerned it never came to this.

So, my Covid journey saw me work more hours than I ever have in my life. But I was one of the lucky ones, I got to look after my patients and have enormous satisfaction for a job well done. I witnessed many colleagues who were drowned by the stress and strain. As part of our MDT, we met regularly with the intensive care consultants who cared for our patients after their big surgery. I witnessed the intense and relentless pressure all these teams were under and wondered how they survived. As far as the Thursday clap goes, I would stand on my doorstep and cry, but no one really knows what it was like unless they were in it, and there really aren't words enough to explain the horror, fear and magnitude of it.

Enough time as has elapsed after retiring and I have now rejoined my patient support group. I still have knowledge to impart and a sympathetic ear so have rejoined the committee. Members include my wonderful friend Tracy, the fabulous Kelly from the upper GI team and group of patients past (See photo 13).

As part of this last week, I attended a Macmillan and Wessex Cancer run information day for cancer sufferers. Three of my old patients were going to attend and speak, so I offered to go as chief cheerleader. It was delightful to be in their company and see them seven, five- and two-years post-surgery. I remember their diagnosis, their highs and their lows and the arc of their recovery. Peter was one of my Covid babies, one of the lucky few who travelled that precarious road of major surgery during the lockdown. I had quite forgotten the extent and the emotion of that terrible time but there in front of the hotel conference room he reminded me.

"If it hadn't been for that angel of a nurse sitting there, we would never have got through it." Peter pointed at me, true to form I cried.

Peter reminded me I had visited him every day for five weeks. Because, for those five long weeks his bed wasn't in the true intensive care, but in a small room off of the operating theatres. The very unique care following his surgery was not being given by the expert nurses, physiotherapists and doctors but a hotch-potch band of staff doing their very best. Nobody asked me to, but I felt I had to check in daily to monitor his progress. He has a wonderful wife and they are very close, it must have been torment for her not to visit. So as with any of my patients who were in the hospital, I would call their families for a daily update. In the carnage and chaos that the NHS was thrown into I adapted, I put my patients needs first, and I ploughed on (See Photo 14), my award for my work through Covid with two fabulous senior surgical nurses.

I hadn't expected to be mentioned in Peter's talk, his unexpected praise, for a moment brought back that dreadful time which I obviously have done well in forgetting. But seeing him standing there, knowing he and his wife have a full and wonderful life together is all the thanks that is needed. I often wonder how I managed to stay in a career that is fraught with stress and overwhelming emotion and just a bloody hard, relentless grind. But Peter summed it up in these few words. You do it because you care. It is a vocation, dress it up with degrees and fancy names, but this is, what it is really all about. If you think nursing is like any other profession, it is not.

Curses

Now I take you into the dark side, the seedy underbelly of the profession. The senior nurses, the managers, the corporate creatures. It has been an unfortunate practice consistent throughout my career - bad nurses rise up. You literally have to kill patients, and not just the accidental one, but be a blatant mass murderer to get yourself booted off the register.

It is even harder now, when we have never been so 'woke'. No more can you tell a nurse they are lazy or incompetent because you yourself will be labelled a bully.

I am aware I may offend some people but I have my views and if they don't tally with yours that's OK. The huge rise in employing nurses whose sole job is to worry about diversity, inclusion and equality is totally pointless. Only this week in the national news, government itself is questioning the post of an equality and diversity lead nurse earning over £90,000 a year. A strong contender for idiotic idea number 9 is the vast amount of time and money the NHS is wasting concerning itself with peoples' proclivities, skin tone, faith or sexual preferences.

I don't care, or judge what-ever you wish to do in life as long as it harms no one else and makes you happy. I attended gay pride with a lesbian friend and even 'pulled' and was randomly kissed full on the mouth by an attractive young blond woman. Far from being affronted or offended as a life-long heterosexual I was delighted that anyone would want to kiss me.

Further-more I have never felt the need to bring the fact that I prefer to sleep with men (well my husband) to work. It is irrelevant to how I do my job. Equally it is irrelevant when I am a patient. I am white, I am British and neither of those things have any relevance to the care I give.

As for religion I have none. It in no way effects the way I treat or respect others. I know not to give a Jehovah's Witness blood. I won't offer a Muslim bacon and if I am in doubt I will ask anything that is pertinent to your care. Again, who you pry to is none of my business.

The first rule of nursing and medicine in general is you treat all patients equally. My mother said to always treat others as you would want to be treated, or how you would want your loved ones to be treated. It is basic, but is universal and part of your training (Well, it was in my day). It is ingrained in you as part of your duty to care so stop going on about it!

If you have a womb, even if you wished you didn't, you will require a gynaecologist to treat you. If you need surgery on said organ, the surgeon won't care if you identify as Brian or Beryl only that the surgery goes well. Medicine is bigger than pronouns.

The NHS was probably the leading industry to employ people from all over the world if they were the best person for the job. Stop talking about it, and get on with your job. I have had the privilege to work with colleagues from all over the planet, it's besides the point. All that matters is you are either competent or not.

In an NHS where patients are left waiting for pain relief because of a lack of qualified nurses, and care is plummeting in an overburdened service, have we all gone mad! We, by profession do not condone bias, these things should not be taking our time, talked about, least of all wasting valuable funds on it.

There has never before been such emphasis placed on well-being and stress. The profession is no more stressful than it ever was, and what still stands true is, if you can't take the stress, work in Marks & Spencer. But with nursing numbers plummeting the biggest stress is that there aren't enough feet on the ground. Get the staff out of offices being paid too much to manage, train and employ enough staff because that is the root of the pressure. The forums are inundated with cries for help from nurses drowning under the pressures of understaffing and failing to give the care that is needed.

Back to the birth of a Curse, in reality a bad student has only a few placements to show themselves, and a whole heap of paperwork and time that assessors don't have. Meaning they slip through the net. Sign them off and you won't have to see them again and then in a blink of an eye they are qualified. Some poor ward or speciality has to employ them, and then the fun starts. Pickings are slim and some job adverts currently receive no applicants. Historically you could pick from a strong bunch but now options are few, and employees can't be fussy.

No one wants to work with them, good support staff move on, good nurses are under the strain of carrying a liability. But the crap nurse has a hide as strong as a rhino and they have no qualms about leaving a trail of tears and bad care in their wake. Their immediate manager is between a rock and a hard place they dare not address it because the bullying card is flapped in their face.

There sadly is one solution, and I am ashamed to say I have done this; the crap nurse must be encouraged to find another job. Of course they will still be a liability, but not on your team. You tell them they will be good at it, it's the perfect role for them. Subsequently with every new job comes a promotion, then, before you know it and certainly before a deserving and dedicated nurse can gain the spot, the 'Curse' as we will refer to her, is now a sister. Money and power make the Curse of formidable beast. The lack of empathy, compassion, understanding and intelligence empower them to slay team spirit, patient care and any joy their staff may once have had.

I have witnessed many Curses in my time and the usual rule applies; the quicker a nurse makes it to the top, the bigger the Curse!

How dare you I hear you cry! And there are the exceptional dedicated, knowledgeable and caring nurses who foolishly think they can be promoted and lead by example. I point you again to photo 14, two fabulous senior nurses and definitely not Curses. What the conscientious nurse hadn't considered is that they have crossed a line. They have crossed the corporate line, whose philosophy, goals, aims and objectives are completely different for the patient facing nurses.

The NHS itself is a wolf in sheep's clothing, no longer the NHS we think it is. It is no longer the service for all that my parents knew and loved, but has been systematically, by stealth, privatised. (See Photo 15), My father in a shop window acting as the patient, they were advertising the new and marvellous NHS. In 2024 it celebrates it's 75 birthday, how times have changed. GPs are now business owners and every medical intervention has its price. The hospitals are businesses, in what realm of stupidity, or greed, was the thought that any business can make a profit when all of your customers are there to take something.

The naive promoted and well-meaning nurse is now a deer in a wood of wolves; they are corporate now; their role is to tow the party line. Chief executives and trust boards - often with not a moment's medical experience between them, - dictate the rules. The deer rails against injustice, stupidity and illogical ideas but this makes her unpopular. Outnumbered and weak it is only a matter of time before she admits defeat and leaves, or conforms. Phrases such as 'you are not a team player', or 'you are being too negative', or 'you are afraid of change', are banded around when any attempt to question a plan that will have a negative impact on the patient.

The Curse on the other hand is rising in the ranks, too unintelligent to be aware of the extent of her bad actions, and the adverse effect on staff and patients. Too emotionally inadequate to communicate effectively, or comprehend the damage they do. It was a conscious decision in my past, way back in my twenties, to never go above the band F - if you are old, junior sister if you are middle-aged or band six if you are a nurse today.

Patients are what float my boat, not spreadsheets, meetings and canoodling with wolves and Curses.

Do I regret this now? Sometimes, because I know I could have managed to do some things better than the Curses I have had to endure. But ultimately my last act as a nurse was to see two of my patients on the wards. I held their hands, I cried with one and I listened, comforted and reassured. I bought knowledge and explanations to their physical issues; comfort to their worries and reassurance to them and their families. I had the best of recompense a nurse can ask for, a hug and a meaningful squeeze of the hand and genuine thanks. Both cancer patients leaving hospital after long and complicated surgery and I had done my job well. But I won't be there to call on Monday to see how they are. I won't be there with a big smile and even a hug in clinic in two weeks time. I might not have been there at the regular support group meetings where I'm greeted as an old friend with patients and their families I have supported for up to 7 years.

A Curse was my undoing. A brown-nosing Curse wanted to impress the chief executive and trust board members. Her grand idea was to take specialist nurses from their offices to staff the wards because of our national shortage of nurses and carers. They even called it 'Tiger teams' WTF! Are we 10? Were we consulted? No! Did these Curses have any idea what job we do or how best to utilise our time? Of course not.

They could have consulted us as professionals and we would have helped, because that's what we do. Instead, they instigate a ludicrous idea and insist you take part

This, my friends, is idiotic idea number ten. For me it was the mother of all stupid ideas and what led to me laying in my bed the next day, having made the decision to not set foot back in that hospital. More and more decisions are being made, that have a detrimental effect on patient care by people who do not consider the patient first but the business plan and their own career. Am I bitter, angry, frustrated, appalled? Yes, to all the above, but having spoken out for what is right for over three decades, I had no fight left in me.

Explaining to my hairdresser why I had abruptly walked out on my job and profession she stated; "Oh that's a shame, but if patients needed feeding and washing, I see why they asked you. Anyway, you would be good at it."

I used an analogy which I think will sum it up, especially to those of you who are not nurses. What I was being ordered to do was equivalent to asking my skilled and highly paid hairdresser to abandon her salon with no notice to her customers for four hours. To go to a random salon that she had never visited and sweep up hair.

Not only does this highlight the total disregard for her skill set and paying her way over what the job entailed, when they could pay half the price and get someone else in, unskilled but happy for the work. I love caring for people and if I didn't care what happened to my cancer patients whilst I was handing out breakfast and washing people I would have enjoyed the experience.

Fundamentally, and the main reason to refuse is the fact that like my role, the hairdresser would four hours later have to return to her salon. Facing a barrage of angry disappointed clients, she would still have to honour and complete the work load in her diary. As a professional (and remember this is not a one-off event but every week) she must complete her obligations and stay until the perm, highlight, restyle and trim are completed to her usual standard.

My clients/patients are calling because instead of highlights they are unable to drink or even swallow their saliva. It could just as well be a frantic wife of a dying patient who doesn't know where to turn. Might it be the patient who has been told yesterday that they probably have cancer but a nurse will call and explain everything.

I don't know about you, but I think the reason I sat in a horrid little office was for a reason. I never went to work for the money or the companionship, they were nice but I was there to offer the best service I could for my cohort of extremely vulnerable patients. Hairdresser or nurse, both professional and the result would always be the same. Immense frustration at misappropriation of skills and budgets. Glaring awareness of failing our client/patient with all the guilt and stress that it brings.

I didn't work my notice, they deserved none. I wrote a lengthy heartfelt resignation and had no reply. And just like that my career was over. I miss being able to use my skills, I miss my patients, and I miss my team but I don't for one minute want to go back.

One of the hospitals head nurses who I included in my resignation email was in the New

Years Honours list 2023. Did she deserve it? I have no idea as I have never met, nor have spoken to her, and she didn't see fit to reply to my resignation.

Things That Stay With You

So as not to end on a negative and leave a bitter taste I will share with you a few things that have always rung true for me.

Firstly, say sorry! It is one of the most powerful words you can utilise when working with people. Whether they are confused, angry, sad or confrontational; sorry is a weapon of self defence. I have often witnessed staff getting defensive when accused or attacked. Nurses sadly, are frequently physically and verbally attacked. As previously stated, this is often derived from fear, pain or frustration.

But never be afraid to say sorry. It will deflate the anger, diffuse the frustration and placate the fearful. The issue or problem may have nothing to do with you but you have the power to de-escalate the situation by simply saying you are sorry that they feel that way. You can't possibly apologise for something out of your control, but you can always acknowledge their pain, frustration and rage. It works like a blanket over flame, connects you to the patient, relative, or even a member of staff come to that.

"I am sorry you feel like that, is there anything I can do?"

It has never failed me and has always resolved conflict that could otherwise have escalated.

Sometimes events will happen that stop with you your whole life. Zooming back to the beginning as a first year on my first ward I contracted flu. I felt terrible and having never been ill since leaving home felt dreadfully homesick. Dragging myself to the internal phone in the nurse's home corridor I called the medical ward I was due to work a night shift on.

"I'm so sorry I have flu and won't be into work."

Apparently, this is not an adequate excuse to be off sick, and I was told with no sympathy. "You have no choice, there is only you and a qualified nurse, get yourself over here."

So, I dragged my feverish body to one of the long old wards. Having missed the handover from the day staff, my colleague for that night took one look at me and put a pillow on the desk in the middle of the ward, and wrapped me in a blanket.

"If I need you, I will have to wake you." And with two paracetamol from the drug trolley, I was just relieved to rest my head and dozed fitfully, oblivious to the rows of beds either side of me. I slept and sweated in my makeshift bed.

The next thing I was aware of, my chair was being shaken and knocked as two ambulance crew manoeuvred a lady onto the bed behind me. I stayed awake long enough to be told she had muscular dystrophy. The lady sat bolt upright in bed, her wizened limbs long and lifeless. She had an exceptionally long thin neck and her expressionless face stared back at me with unblinking eyes.

My main concern was nursing my own high-temperature, and in a dreamlike state I dozed again into my pillow. I can't remember how long it was until I was roughly shaken awake.

"Our new admission is dead!"

Trying to wake myself and see clearly, I rubbed my eyes and looking behind me. I saw the lady, eyes still wide, sitting upright and dead. Her last moments on this earth were spent watching my back as I slept. Could I have altered her death? No. Could I have sat and comforted her? Yes. I will never know if she was fearful, or if she wanted to scream at me to wake up.

What was done, was done. I was genuinely too unwell to have done anything differently. But that nightshift has haunted and affected any nightshift I have worked and often appears in my dreams ever since. It affected me in such a profound way that never again did I sleep or rest when working on a nightshift. I could never be that nurse who hunkered down in the dayroom with a pillow, blankets and try to catch an hour or two sleep. In nursing homes, it is common practice for the staff to doze in chairs and nap unless disturbed by a bell. I believe I was universally hated when working nights in nursing homes because of my constant prowling and checking of patients. I was always very considerate and tried not to wake the patients, but my fellow staff, I'm sure, wished I would just put my head down.

If ever I am worried about work, whatever the role, there is a recurring dream that has stayed with me all these years. My hope, now I am retired, is that I will be free of it. In the dream I will be working a nightshift, often in a hospital, but sometimes just for a change it will be a nursing home. The detail and the length of the dream varies but it always ends the same. I have got through the hideous witching hour of 4am (if you have never worked nights, it is the time you would pay anything just to lay down and sleep). With daybreak comes the blessed sight of the early shift reluctantly making their way to relieve you. It is always at this moment that the member of the new shift asks after a patient that I do not know.

The heart lurching, stomach churning, dread that you have failed. Opening the door of the ward you had not known existed, finding the four bedded area that no one has tended all night. There is always a combination of desperate patients that have either fallen out of bed, are floating in their own urine and faeces, or worst of all, stone cold dead.

Whether this dream was planted in my mind because of that poor lady I will never know. But I remember her name, I remain apologetic for not doing more, and I am convinced this incident made me the hyper vigilant nurse I have always been. So maybe, from a negative act, there is a positive outcome.

Conclusion

It is with great sadness I see my beloved profession fail; it is truly at breaking point. The Curses hatched their plan and laid it before us is a *fait accomplis* but I'm too old and too tired, I had the T-shirt in the 80s and can't bear to accept another idiotic idea wrapped up in a corporate ribbon of change and progress. I witnessed Project 2000 to create more intelligent nurses, a disaster. Then nursing was taught at university to raise our profile and raise wages, made not a jot of difference, only lessened our training and professionalism (See photo 16). I have no degree, it has never been needed. Without doubt they were all stupid ideas, they failed, failed the poor students who now need to sell a kidney to afford their training. Fundamentally and much more importantly they have failed the patients.

So, I said no, no thank you to your order to spend four hours on any ward of your choosing as an emergency washing service. I can care, wash, dress wounds better than a lot of other staff, if the shabby state of my cancer patients on the wards was a measure. But there is a principle here people, you are leaving my patients unattended and for those four hours who cares for my cancer patients? CNSs don't have shifts, no-one else is covering my patients and when a specialist nurse drops the ball there is no one else to know it has been dropped, let alone pick it up and run with it. Can a nurse of my experience say no I hear you ask, the answer of course is no.

 Apparently, my leaving sent little ripples around the hospital and some nurses were quoted as saying "No, no you can't make me. I'll do an Anne!"

 As far as I know this particular idiotic idea was shelved, but without doubt there will be more. For now, I leave it to others to shout down the stupid, and stand up for what is right. I'm sure they will be condemned for being unhelpful and disruptive, but I hope at least there are people out there whose first priority is the patient.

 It is now October 2024 and hoping to get this book uploaded for sale. I have wasted the requisite months researching agents and submitting my work. They ask you not to blanket submit but research each company and find the right 'fit' for you – so you do. They explain they are so busy and important, they may take 12 weeks to come back to you. The daily checking of emails for ten weeks and the o so polite rejections trickle in. I am not bitter I am a realist, I am grateful for the delay as yesterday I had an epiphany and I can share it with you.

I listened in to a radio show discussing the Covid enquiry and sobbed as I drove, the accounts of Intensive care professionals brought back the trauma of it all. I had also watched a piece on PTSD this week. With time and hindsight and the complete lack of consideration, counselling or care from the health service at the time I had the huge realisation that I suspect Covid had left me with a level of PTSD.

With the trauma and damage of Covid nicely tucked away with all the other ghastly things nursing has inflicted on me; the threat of forcing me to work on the wards yet again, ripped off the scab keeping all the bile and muck contained, and it spilt out. The head nurse, who's idea it was that pushed me over the brink, accused me of being aggressive. If she were any sort of nurse, she should have recognised the distress and fear I was exhibiting. The radio presenter was shocked that following

Covid staff were not offered counselling, at least this gave me a good laugh.

I would still have resigned on the principle of not doing a stupid thing, but had it not been for Covid my leaving may have not been so traumatic.

So here we are a whistle stop tour of 37 years of nursing. The highs, the lows, the joys, the pain. I have long considered writing this book but could not envisage the end. What the final chapter would be. The answer came in a blaze of principle and a stand for what is right, and a realisation I could take, nor give any more - it felt good. Before this book is printed the nurse's home at Epsom will have been demolished, what a waste. I will take it as a sign, a sign that it is time for me to let my registration go.

If we are so desperate, and believe me the NHS is, that people are going unwashed and unfed; swallow your corporate pride and ask families to come in and wash and feed their loved ones because it really has come to that. If you can't safely staff wards, close them, cancel surgery, appointments and pool your resources where they must be. But this is not the corporate way, it does not fit the business plan. Everything is new and shiny, but like a Stepford Wife, behind the facade patients care is compromised, staff morale is at an all-time low and the NHS teeters on the brink.

It has been two years since I walked away, and I am very content. Life has a way of working out and I have been glad to have the time for my dear friend who was diagnosed shortly after I left my job with advanced cancer. I have used these months to be her support and guide her through the complex journey. The view from the patient side is even more frightening, but that's a whole different story.

Sharing this, my short rant and the testament of experiences in my chosen profession, I hope it has given an insight. It is unashamedly personal and I care not what critique I receive. I hope to have shown the diversity and complexity of the job like no other, a job I loved and sometimes loathed, but I was always immeasurably proud to call myself a nurse. As I leave, my hopes and dreams are for the tide to turn for our collapsing NHS. For it to rally, and once again be the envy of the world, and fend off the wave of privatisation.

To the young nurses I have worked with, keep going! It was their eagerness to learn, their insights and thoughts that were, and are, the hope for tomorrow. There are people out there who want to care, who need to be taught how to do it properly. I only hope the profession can retrench and bring back a nurse training better suited for the practical and let us not forget, vocational job that is nursing. Not the financially crippled, disenchanted and exhausted workforce we currently have.

I stated at the beginning I wanted to capture the essence of what nursing is, but it is one million small things. It is an enigma, and if you had to describe it, so many words are negative. It is certainly at times; loathsome, heartbreaking, harrowing, exhausting and unpleasant. But to keep going a nurse must cling to the good. This may be a moment in a long shift, but it is recognition for your efforts, and recompense for all your hard work. It may be the smile on the face of someone you helped to stand who didn't think they would be able to. It may be the thanks of the relative for the care you have shown their loved one. Ultimately the biggest reward will never be financial, but the knowledge that you helped, the true definition of job satisfaction.

I know what good care is. I only hope there are people out there who can deliver it for me and mine when we are in need. I have worked with countless wonderful colleagues over the years, too many to mention. All of whom have dedicated so much to care for others. There have probably been thirty over the years who should really have been in a different profession, and as I am very poor at masking my displeasure, they probably know who they are.

I have laughed and cried in equal measure in a career caring for others. Being a nurse is truly one of the hardest things but the rewards are carried in your heart, with the knowledge of a job well done.

"Hello, my name is Anne" will never be used in a professional capacity again. I will always have the heart of a nurse it is hard wired in. Whether it is volunteering at a support group or coming to a rescue of a very sick man at a joisting match recently all I have learnt is still there. Thankfully the nightmares and strain are gone and I am relieved and happy to not renew my registration.

If anyone reading thinks I want to be a nurse, good for you, and as the Americans would say 'have at it!'

Ultimately, I know my parents would be proud, and that makes it all worthwhile.

Printed in Great Britain
by Amazon